POLISI V. CLARK AND PARKER & GOULD

ADVANCED CASE FILE

SECOND EDITION

POLISI V. CLARK AND PARKER & GOULD

ADVANCED CASE FILE

SECOND EDITION

Anthony J. Bocchino
Jack E. Feinberg Professor of Litigation
Temple University Beasley School of Law

David A. Sonenshein
I. Herman Stern Professor of Law
Temple University Beasley School of Law

Graphics and electronic files by
Frank D. Rothschild

NATIONAL INSTITUTE FOR TRIAL ADVOCACY

© 2001 by the National Institute for Trial Advocacy, Inc.

Printed in the United States of America. All rights reserved.

Bocchino, Anthony J. and David A. Sonenshein, *Polisi v. Simon Clark and Parker & Gould Case File*, 2d ed., (NITA, 2001)

ISBN 1-55681-727-4
ISBN 13: 978-1-55681-727-4

FBA0727

1/01   04/08   12/09

ACKNOWLEDGMENTS

We thank our colleagues, Professor Laura Little and Professor Alice Abreu for their invaluable assistance in the production of this case file. We also thank the participants in the inaugural class of Temple Law School's LL.M. in Trial Advocacy who worked through this file as part of their program and provided insight into improving the realism of the case file. We also are grateful to our Civil Procedure students who utilized another form of this case file and also provided helpful suggestions on its improvement.

Finally, we are indebted to Jerome Staller, Ph.D., and Stephanie Thomas, Ph.D., of the Center for Forensic Economic Studies in Philadelphia, who wrote the expert witness reports that appear in this file.

AJB
DAS

POLISI V. CLARK AND PARKER & GOULD

CASE FILE

Contents

How to Use the CD-ROM

This book includes a CD-ROM that contains a PowerPoint® slide show, digital copies of exhibits and expert reports, and video clips for this case. Those who are familiar with the use of CDs as file storage media do not need to read this section, as this CD is standard in all respects. Those who are new to the use of CDs should review and follow these instructions.

This CD can be used in three ways—to examine the files that it contains; to work with these files by editing, supplementing, or copying them; and to display files for third persons in an office, classroom, or courtroom setting. If you are just perusing the files, you can use them efficiently on the CD. If you are working with or displaying the files for others, you will want to copy them to the hard drive of your computer so that they will play more quickly and smoothly. Each method is explained below.

TO VIEW THE FILES ON THE CD

1. Insert the CD into the CD drive of your computer.

2. Go to the Windows Desktop. This is the screen display that contains the icons for basic Windows functions as well as for software programs that have been installed on the computer.

3. Double click on the My Computer icon, which looks like this.

   This displays icons for each of the drives on your computer (usually A, C, D, and so on) together with some other basic controls. You are going to use the icon for the CD drive, which looks like this.

   Wait for a few seconds while the computer identifies the CD. It will change to show that it can read the disk by displaying a name under the icon like this.

4. Double click on the icon for the CD drive. This displays icons for each of the folders that the CD contains, which are Exhibit Scans, Expert Scans, and Slides.

5. Double click on the Slides folder. This displays a PowerPoint icon plus a number of video clip icons.

6. To run the PowerPoint slide show for the case, double click on the PowerPoint file with the extension .ppt that is inside the folder.

   PowerPoint will open the slide show automatically and then stop, waiting for further instructions.

7. Click on the Slide Show icon on the bottom left of the screen to go into "play mode." This is the set of instructions under which PowerPoint will go from one slide to the next so that you can look at all the slides in the collection.

The screen display looks like this.

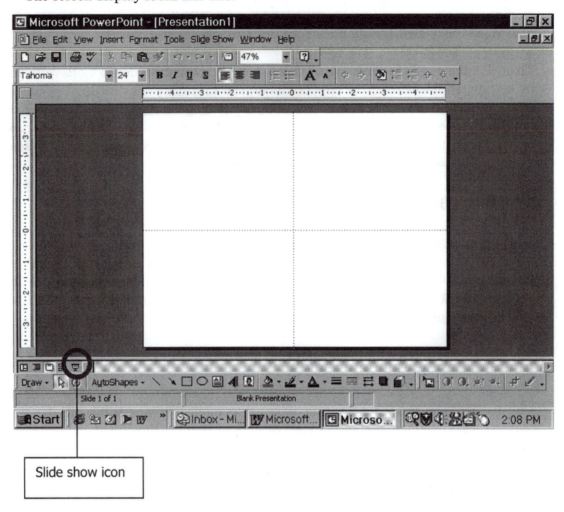

Slide show icon

The first slide of the presentation will appear, which will be a black slide.

- To display any other slide in the slide show, simply type the slide number (**NOT** the exhibit number) as shown in the thumbnail printouts at the back of the case file and hit the "Enter" key.

- To see the next slide in order, click the left mouse or press the space bar.

- To go back one slide, press the "Page Up" key.

- To go to any other slide, type the slide number and hit the Enter key.

- To play animations (if the slide contains any), either left click the mouse or press the space bar to initiate each animation.

- To take projected images off the screen or monitor and go back to a neutral blank screen, type in "1" plus "Enter" to return to the first slide.

- To play the video clips, bring up the slide you want by typing the slide number and hitting "Enter," then move the mouse cursor into the image [you might need to move the mouse around rapidly for a second or two to see the cursor on the screen]. Once in the video image, the cursor will change from a pointed arrow into a little white hand. That is your signal that the video is ready to play. Left click once and the video will play. You can stop and start the video with a left mouse click so long as the cursor remains inside the image.

- To display Q & A text in synch with a video, start the video (as above), then put the cursor outside the image [it will change back to an arrow] and click the left mouse to bring up each Q & A in synch with the video. It is simple and takes little practice to master.

TO TRANSFER THE FILES TO YOUR COMPUTER'S HARD DRIVE

For best results, it is highly recommended that you download the files from the CD to your hard drive. The slide shows and video clips will play faster and much more smoothly this way. The easiest way to accomplish this is as follows.

1. Open the CD in My Computer.

2. Click on Edit on the top toolbar.

3. From the drop-down menu, click "Select All," which will highlight all of the folders on the CD.

4. Right click on those selected folders.

5. Select the "Send to" option and, from that menu, click on "My Documents." the folders will be copied to your hard drive in the My Documents folder.

To answer other questions you may have, please refer to *PowerPoint for Litigators*, Siemer, Rothschild, Stein, and Solomon (NITA, 2000).

INTRODUCTION

1. This is gender discrimination and defamation case based on a claim by the Plaintiff that she was denied partnership in the Defendant law firm, Parker & Gould (P & G), because she terminated a sexual relationship with the Defendant, Clark. She also claims gender discrimination based on a sexual harassment claim against the Defendant, Clark, and a hostile work environment claim against both Defendants.

2. This case file is designed for advanced advocacy training and involves difficult legal and factual issues for jury resolution. It also requires the examination of expert witnesses.

3. The parties have stipulated that all documents are authentic and meet the requirements of the Original Documents Rule. Other requirements for admissibility must be established by offering counsel.

4. This case file is completely fictitious and any resemblance to any person living or dead is coincidental and should not be misconstrued.

IN THE UNITED STATES DISTRICT COURT
FOR THE DISTRICT OF NITA

MARGARET POLISI   :
                                   :
        Plaintiff   :   CIVIL ACTION NO.
                                   :   2002-4678
        v.   :
                                   :
                                   :   JURY TRIAL DEMANDED
                                   :
SIMON CLARK   :
                                   :
        and   :
                                   :
PARKER & GOULD   :
                                   :
        Defendants   :

COMPLAINT

PARTIES

        1.   Plaintiff, Margaret Polisi, is a female, adult individual, who is a citizen of Nita

and of the United States. She resides in Nita City, Nita.

        2(a).   Defendant, Parker & Gould, is a partnership organized under the laws of the State

of Nita, engaged in the practice of law in Nita, with its offices at Four Independence Square, Nita

City, Nita.

        2(b).   Defendant, Parker & Gould, is an employer within the meaning of Section 701(b)

of Title VII of the Civil Rights Act of 1964, as amended, 42 U.S.C. § 2000e(b), in that it engages

in an industry affecting commerce and has had fifteen (15) or more employees for each working

day in each of twenty (20) or more calendar weeks in the current or pending calendar year.

3(a).   Defendant, Simon Clark, is a male, adult individual who is a citizen of Nita and the United States. He resides in Nita City, Nita.

3(b).   Defendant, Simon Clark, at all times material to this lawsuit, was and continues to be, a partner in the Defendant, Parker & Gould, and an agent of Parker & Gould within the meaning of 42 U.S.C. § 2000e(b).

JURISDICTION AND VENUE

4.   Plaintiff invokes this court's jurisdiction pursuant to 28 U.S.C. § 1331, 42 U.S.C. § 2000e-5(f)(3) and invokes Supplemental Jurisdiction pursuant to 28 U.S.C. § 1367. This action arises pursuant to 42 U.S.C. § 2000e et seq., Title VII of the Civil Rights Act of 1964, as amended.

5.   All conditions precedent to the filing of this action have been satisfied in that the Equal Employment Opportunity Commission of the United States issued its Right to Sue notice on December 28, 2001.

6.   Venue is appropriate in the District of Nita because the defendants both reside in the State of Nita, the claims arose there, and the defendants may both be served with process there.

CLAIM I

Violation of the Civil Rights Act of 1964 — Gender Discrimination

7.   Plaintiff graduated from Nita University Law School and passed the Nita bar examination in 1994.

8.   In 1994, Defendant, Parker & Gould, hired Plaintiff as a litigation associate in the law firm, where Plaintiff worked for seven years prior to her being forced to resign her position in the firm.

9.   In June of 2000, Defendant Clark initiated a sexual relationship with the Plaintiff while she was an associate, working for him on the business of the Defendant, Parker and Gould.

10.   In January of 2001, Plaintiff terminated the sexual relationship with Defendant, Clark.

11.   Although Plaintiff received excellent evaluations of her work over the period of her employment with Defendant, Parker & Gould, Plaintiff was rejected for partnership while male associates who were less qualified than Plaintiff were accepted for partnership with the Defendant, Parker & Gould, in 2001.

12.   Plaintiff was rejected for partnership in the Defendant firm because she terminated a sexual relationship with her supervisor, Defendant, Simon Clark, in violation of Plaintiff's rights under Title VII of the Civil Rights Act of 1964, as amended, 42 U.S.C. § 2000e et seq.

CLAIM II

Violation of the Civil Rights Act of 1964 —

Quid Pro Quo Sexual Harassment

13.   Plaintiff incorporates by reference paragraphs 1 through 10 hereof, all of which amount to quid pro quo sexual harassment in violation of Title VII of the Civil Rights Act of 1964, 42 U.S.C. § 2000e, et seq.

CLAIM III

Violation of the Civil Rights Act of 1964 —

Hostile Working Environment

14.   Plaintiff incorporates by reference paragraph 1 through 11 hereof.

15.   Defendant Clark, while Plaintiff's supervisor, sexually harassed Plaintiff by, on numerous occasions, making unwelcome sexual advances to Plaintiff, culminating in a sexually intimate affair, all of which created and imposed on Plaintiff a sexually hostile and abusive

working environment in violation of Plaintiff's rights pursuant to Title VII of the Civil Rights Act of 1964, as amended, 42 U.S.C. § 2000e, et seq.

WHEREFORE, Plaintiff prays that this Court will:

A.   Issue a declaratory judgment declaring that the actions of Defendants, Parker & Gould, and Clark, as set forth in this Complaint, violated Plaintiff's rights under Title VII of the Civil Rights Act of 1964, as amended, 42 U.S.C. § 2000e et seq.

B.   Enjoin and restrain Defendants Parker & Gould and Clark and all other persons acting on behalf of, or in concert with, them from engaging in such unlawful practices.

C.   Enter judgment in favor of Plaintiff, and against Defendants, Parker & Gould, and Clark, for back pay in the amount of wages and fringe benefits it is determined that Plaintiff lost as a result of Defendants' unlawful conduct, together with interest.

D.   Enter judgment in favor of Plaintiff and against Defendants, Parker & Gould, and Clark, reinstating plaintiff to the position she would have had absent Defendants' unlawful conduct. In the alternative, award plaintiff front pay in the amount of wages and benefits it is determined that Plaintiff is likely to lose because of Defendants' unlawful conduct.

E.   Enter judgment in favor of Plaintiff, and against Defendants for compensatory damages, including but not limited to, damages for mental anguish and humiliation, together with interest.

F.   Award Plaintiff reasonable attorneys' fees together with the costs of this action.

G.   Award such other and further legal and equitable relief as may be appropriate to redress fully the deprivation of Plaintiff's rights, to prevent their recurrence in the future and to protect other Parker & Gould employees from such unlawful behavior.

CLAIM IV

Defamation

16.   Plaintiff incorporates herein by reference paragraphs 1 through 15 hereof.

17.   Following the Plaintiff's rejection for partnership by the Defendant, Parker & Gould, Plaintiff applied for attorney positions with other law firms.

18.   When Defendant, Parker & Gould, was asked by at least two of the above-mentioned prospective employers for its opinion regarding Plaintiff's personality and abilities, Defendant, Clark, maliciously responded with false and slanderous statements, which defamed Plaintiff in her personal and professional reputation.

19.   The false statements made by Defendant, Clark, were made with the express, implied or apparent authority of Defendant, Parker & Gould, and Defendant, Parker & Gould, ratified those statements by not repudiating them.

20.   As a result of the false and slanderous statements maliciously made by Defendant, Clark, and ratified by Defendant, Parker & Gould, Plaintiff has suffered substantial emotional distress, mental anguish and pain and suffering; as well as damage to her personal and professional reputation and earning capacity.

WHEREFORE, Plaintiff demands judgment against Defendants, Parker & Gould, and Clark, for compensatory damages in an amount in excess of $1,000,000.

clearly truth matters

JURY DEMAND

Plaintiff demands a jury trial for all claims triable by a jury.

Respectfully submitted,

David Darrow, Esquire
1500 Main Street
Nita City, Nita 10076

Dated: February 2, 2002.

VERIFICATION

I, Margaret Polisi, am the plaintiff in the above-captioned action. I have read this complaint and verify that the allegations in it are true.

Margaret Polisi, Esq.

Signed and sworn before me
this 2nd day of February, 2002.

Notary Public

IN THE UNITED STATES DISTRICT COURT
FOR THE DISTRICT OF NITA

MARGARET POLISI	:	
	:	
Plaintiff	:	CIVIL ACTION NO.
	:	2002-4678
v.	:	
	:	
	:	JURY TRIAL DEMANDED
	:	
SIMON CLARK	:	
	:	
and	:	
	:	
PARKER & GOULD	:	
	:	
Defendants	:	

ANSWER OF
DEFENDANTS SIMON CLARK
and PARKER & GOULD

By way of answer, Defendants, Simon Clark and Parker & Gould, respond to Plaintiff's

allegations as follows:

1.   Admit.

2(a).   Admit.

2(b).   Admit.

3(a).   Admit.

3(b).   Admit.

4.   Admit.

5.   Admit.

6.   Admit.

7.   Admit.

8.   Admit the Defendant law firm hired Plaintiff as an associate in 1994 and that Plaintiff worked at the firm for seven years before resigning her position.

9.   Deny that the Defendant Clark initiated the relationship. The relationship was mutually, freely and willingly entered into by the Plaintiff and the Defendant Clark.

10.   Admit.

11.   Admit that Plaintiff was rejected for partnership, but deny that Plaintiff received excellent evaluations over the period of her employment with the Defendant law firm.

12.   Denied.

13.   Deny all allegations incorporated by reference which were heretofore denied, and admit those allegations already admitted. Deny the allegation of quid pro quo sexual harassment.

14.   Deny all allegations incorporated by reference which were heretofore denied, and admit those allegations already admitted.

15.   Denied.

16.   Deny all allegations incorporated by reference which were heretofore denied, and admit those allegations already admitted.

17.   Defendants have insufficient knowledge to admit or deny.

18.   Denied.

19.   Denied.

20.   Denied.

For the Defendants,
Simon Clark and
Parker & Gould,

Jane Jackson

Jane Jackson, Esq.

DEPOSITION OF MARGARET POLISI

1   My name is Maggie Polisi. I live at 7010 Greenhill Rd. in Nita City. I am forty-one years old
2 and the single parent of two children: Dave, who is twenty-one and a senior at Nita University, and
3 Maureen, who is nineteen and a sophomore at Conwell College in the northwest part of the state.
4 Until December 15th of 2001, I was a lawyer with the firm of Parker & Gould in Nita City, at which
5 time I was forced out of the law firm. Since then I have accepted a position as an Associate Professor
6 of Law at Nita University School of Law where I teach Civil Procedure, Evidence, and a seminar
7 in Complex Civil Litigation. I began this position as a tenure line faculty member in September of
8 2002. During the spring semester, 2002, I was an Adjunct Professor at the law school. I was hired
9 as a full-time member of the faculty when a slot came open for the 2002–2003 academic year.
10
11   I was born and raised in Wallingford, Connecticut, where I attended the public schools. In
12 1980 I graduated from Lyman Hall High School and enrolled at the University of Pennsylvania in
13 Philadelphia, where I majored in Political Science. During my freshman year I met Gregory Meyers,
14 who was an MBA student at the Wharton School at Penn. We dated very seriously and in the spring
15 of my freshman year, I became pregnant with my son, David. Greg and I married that summer, and
16 he took a job with the Nita Fidelity Bank in their foreign investment division. I transferred from
17 Penn to the University of Nita where I continued my studies.
18
19   My daughter Maureen was born in 1984, one month after I graduated from Nita University.
20 I was a good student and graduated summa cum laude and was elected to Phi Beta Kappa. Greg and
21 I decided that it would be best for the kids if I stayed home with them while they were little, so I put
22 my career on hold. As it turned out, Greg and I were not meant to be married to each other. His trips
23 to Europe became longer and longer, and after a while, I didn't even mind. In 1986, we divorced and
24 Greg moved to Europe to work for an investment house there. I needed to work to help support my
25 kids, but also to keep my sanity.
26
27   Given my undergraduate degree in political science, I had no particular job skills. I always
28 had an interest in the law, so at the encouragement of a good friend of mine, I applied to a number
29 of law firms to work as a paralegal. I received a number of offers, but chose to go with Parker &
30 Gould. P & G appeared to be the most flexible in terms of giving me time to care for my kids when
31 I was needed. They were also willing to assign me to cases that did not take me out of town for
32 anything more that a night or two. They understood that I was a single mother, and that to send me
33 out of town was a hardship. No other firm was willing to give me such assurances, so I went with
34 P & G.
35
36   P & G is a large law firm that does the full range of legal work available in the city. The firm
37 now has approximately 330 lawyers, seventy-five of whom are partners. At the time I went to work
38 for P & G as a paralegal, it was one of the largest law firms in Nita City, but only had about seventy-
39 five lawyers. I was assigned to the litigation section of the firm. The firm also has a corporate
40 section, a tax section, and an estates section.
41
42   I did work for many of the partners at the firm, but in 1988 I was assigned to work on a large
43 commercial case involving several of the biggest banks in Nita City. The partner in charge of that
44 case was Simon Clark, and I worked very closely with him and with Cliff Fuller (who at the time

1   was a mid-level associate with the firm) for a period of approximately two years. By the time the
2   case came to trial, in January of 1990, I was selected as one of the trial paralegals to work on the
3   case. Simon was apparently pleased with my work because I received a substantial bonus and a pay
4   raise when we won the case at trial, and settled it very favorably in lieu of an appeal.
5
6   Simon Clark has always had a reputation in the firm as a womanizer. I was warned by a
7   number of the more senior paralegals as well as some of the women associates to watch out for him
8   when I joined the firm. They told me that Simon was in a very unhappy marriage, and that he used
9   this fact as an entreé with a number of women in the office, both paralegals and lawyers. Apparently
10 he had promised a number of young women that he would leave his wife to be with them, but that
11 never happened. In the end, the women would either quit the firm or be fired, and Simon would go
12 on to his next conquest.
13
14   I'll have to admit, that during the bank case in 1988 through 1990, I worked very closely with
15 Simon for long hours and in close quarters, and he never really came on to me. There was some
16 innocent flirting on his part, but maybe because of his reputation, or maybe because he reminded me
17 of my husband, I steered clear of him. I don't know if he was interested in a personal relationship
18 with me at the time, but as I said, I never really responded to his flirting and he never made any
19 inappropriate advances other than from time to time, when talking with me, he would touch me. For
20 example, when he was reading something over my shoulder, he would put his hands on my
21 shoulders. Although this bothered me, I never said anything because, after all, he was the boss and
22 even though I was uncomfortable with the physical contact, it did not seem to be overtly sexual in
23 nature.
24
25   As it turned out, he apparently was involved with a woman associate at the firm, one who
26 was also working on the case. Her name is Susan McGinty. Susan left the firm some time after the
27 bank case. I understand that she now practices law in Philadelphia. The word is that when Simon
28 refused to leave his wife, Susan put her foot down, and the end result was that she was forced to
29 leave the firm.
30
31   During the bank case, Simon was very complimentary of my work. He often said things to
32 the effect that I was the equal of many of the associates who were working on the case. Once he even
33 kidded Cliff Fuller in front of me that I was going to take Cliff's place. In fact, it was Simon Clark
34 who encouraged me to attend law school. He recommended that I leave the firm and go to school
35 full time, but by that time, my ex-husband's child support payments were sporadic at best, and it was
36 an economic necessity for me to continue to work. I applied to, and was accepted, as an Evening
37 Division law student at Nita University School of Law and began classes in the fall of 1990. Both
38 Simon and Cliff (who was a graduate of Nita law school) wrote letters of recommendation for me.
39 I'm sure they were helpful because my application was a little late and I still was accepted.
40
41   I continued to work at P & G during my law school years. The firm was very good about
42 accommodating my law school schedule, and allowed me to take some time off during exams and
43 make it up later. I also was given permission to use the law firm facilities for my research and
44 writing projects during non-work hours. During the entire time I was in law school Simon Clark
45 showed a good deal of interest in me and my legal career. When I made Dean's list in my first
46 semester of law school he was very complimentary and offered to take me out to dinner to celebrate.
47 Because I was so busy, between work, school, and my kids, I turned him down for dinner, but did

1 agree to go to lunch. At lunch he was very charming and appeared to be genuinely interested in me,
2 my kids, and my career. He said that I should be sure to make some time for myself and although
3 this was good advice, the time just wasn't there.
4
5   Simon's apparent professional interest in me continued throughout my law school career. He
6 was always available to discuss a problem I had with my law school work, or with a case I was
7 working on at the firm. Although his habit of touching on the arm or shoulder when we were talking
8 embarrassed me, I never said anything to him because the touching, although unwanted, was not,
9 as I said earlier, overtly sexual. After my first year at law school, during which I achieved top 5
10 percent grades, I was promoted in the firm to a position as a law clerk. The work I did as a law clerk
11 in the beginning was not much different than my paralegal work, but as I became more sophisticated
12 in the law, so did my assignments. Although I did not receive formal evaluations as a law clerk at
13 P & G, I was rehired each year, and my pay was increased on a regular basis.
14
15   In addition, unlike most of the law clerks, I did receive bonuses each year. It was explained
16 to me that since I would have received bonuses as a paralegal, that the firm had decided that I would
17 continue to be part of the bonus compensation program at the firm. To tell you the truth, I was quite
18 surprised when I did receive a bonus at the end of the year in which I became a law clerk, because
19 I knew that the law clerks did not normally get bonuses. I was given my bonus check by Simon
20 Clark. I remember that I had just had to do some roof repairs on my small house, and that it looked
21 like we were going to have a lean Christmas when he gave me the check. The bonus was something
22 like $2,000 and it could not have come at a better time. I was so excited that I gave Simon a big hug.
23 I remember he made some comment like, "with that reaction, I wish we could have given you more."
24 What he said embarrassed me, but I really didn't think much of it the time. I just let go of him, and
25 thanked him. He told me that he had gone to bat for me on the bonus, and that I was the only law
26 clerk to receive one. I thanked him again, and that was that.
27
28   I did very well in law school. I always made Dean's list, and according to the percentile
29 rankings, my grades were always in the top 5 percent which was the highest percentile reported. I
30 was selected for the law review. I had a note published in my second year, a comment published in
31 my third year and in my fourth year, I was selected to be one of the Articles Editors.
32
33   During the four years of law school, I did some assignments on Simon Clark's cases and he
34 always seemed to be pleased with my work. He did ask me out to dinner on a number of occasions
35 to either celebrate some success of mine at the law school or the winning of a case of his that we
36 worked on together. I always declined because of my schedule, but we did go out to lunch several
37 times. Simon would flirt with me, telling me how attractive I was or by making comments like "if
38 I weren't a married man, I'd be camped out at your doorstep," and "if I were only ten years younger,
39 I'd fly away with you to a desert island." Although I was embarrassed by his behavior, I just put it
40 off to his being from another era, and just sloughed him off by making a little joke or ignoring him.
41 Also, because I thought that, even though his comments were embarrassing to me, he did not mean
42 anything by the comments, I thought that any protest on my part would look silly, and he might view
43 me as an "hysterical woman."
44
45   During the four years I was at the law school, Simon Clark's stock rose steadily with the
46 firm. He was obviously one of the firm's best litigators and trial lawyers, and was very well regarded
47 professionally within the firm. It was generally known in the firm that Simon was responsible for

1 attracting and keeping some of the firm's best clients. It was probably because of his talent that his
2 extramarital affairs with both paralegals and associates were so easily tolerated. It might also have
3 been that the firm didn't care about his personal life, so long as he continued to succeed as a lawyer.
4 I really can't understand why the firm put up with his behavior, but it did. At any rate, the rumors
5 of his philandering never ceased, and Simon went through a number of fairly public affairs within
6 the firm while I was in law school.
7
8   I know for a fact that he had a six-month relationship with Ellen Dorsen, who was a paralegal
9 with the firm. This was in 1991. She spoke openly of her weekends with Simon, and the places they
10 went together. When the affair ended, Ellen took it quite hard. A number of the other paralegals were
11 very hard on her, given the way she flaunted her relationship with Simon, and it affected her work.
12 She was eventually fired by the firm. I also know that Simon had affairs with two women associates,
13 Karen Newman in 1992, and Carol Merritt in 1993. I know this because they were assigned to work
14 on two different cases with Simon, both of which I was assigned to as a law clerk.
15
16   Karen was a third-year associate and in her late twenties at the time of her fling with Simon.
17 She initially sort of took the whole thing in stride. When the affair ended after about a month, she
18 confided in me about it. She said that Simon had made some statements about leaving his wife, but
19 that Karen knew he was lying, so she ended the relationship. Over the next several months Karen
20 complained to me, and anyone else who would listen, about how her work assignments had gotten
21 pretty bad and that rather than being assigned to the high profile commercial cases, as she had been
22 in the recent past, she was being asked to work on some divorce matters for some of our business
23 clients. She also complained that she was having a hard time keeping her billable hours up because
24 she wasn't getting assigned enough work. I know one of the people she complained to at the time
25 was Cliff Fuller, who by that time was a well-respected young partner at the firm, and was known
26 to be Simon Clark's protege.
27
28   The divorce cases were not considered great cases in the firm at that time because they were
29 only handled because the client was a business client, not because the firm valued this type of
30 practice. Karen held on for about six months, but eventually left the firm for a job with a smaller
31 firm. At the time she told me that she believed that her dumping Simon was the reason for her bad
32 assignments or lack of assignments and that she decided to leave the firm before "they" could
33 damage her reputation. At the time I thought she was overreacting, but given what happened to me,
34 my guess is she did the right thing for herself at the time. I have seen Karen every once in a while
35 since she left the firm. When this whole thing happened to me, she somehow heard about it and
36 asked me to lunch. She commiserated with me. Her basic comment was that Simon appeared to be
37 up to his old tricks. Although she didn't name names, she told me there were a number of women
38 (either paralegals or lawyers) in the city who had been forced out of P & G after their relationships
39 ended with Simon Clark.
40
41   Carol Merritt's situation was more complicated. At the time she started her affair with Simon,
42 she was a fourth-year associate, about thirty years old, and married. She fell head over heels in love
43 with Simon while working on a case with him. Their affair lasted a good six months. About three
44 months into the affair, she got so serious that she left her husband. I had a conversation with her
45 about Simon before she left her husband, and warned her about Simon's reputation. I even suggested
46 she contact Karen Newman or talk to Cliff Fuller. She assured me that Simon was going to leave his
47 wife and marry her; that he was just waiting for the right time, but that it would be soon. As it turned

1   out, Simon never did leave his wife, and when the case they were working on together ended, he
2   terminated his relationship with Carol abruptly. Carol ended up taking about a month off, and came
3   back to the firm only long enough to pack up her office and move out. I found out she was leaving
4   from Rachel Levin, who was Charles Milton's secretary with whom I was friendly at the time. I
5   talked to Carol at Rachel's suggestion. She thanked me for trying to be a good friend when I warned
6   her about Simon. She also told me that her husband had taken her back and that the two of them were
7   moving to Washington, D.C. She said that even though Simon had been a jerk, that he had given her
8   a great recommendation, and that she was going to work for a good firm in D.C.
9
10   I think that Carol's, as well as Karen's, experiences were consistent with Simon Clark's
11 normal behavior. I don't think that he is an evil man, but I do think that he does evil things. He has
12 a fatal flaw in that he cannot be satisfied with one woman, or at least, not for long. But when he's
13 done with them, or they're done with him, he doesn't want them around. I don't know whether he
14 knows or cares about how devastating being treated like that can be. My conclusions about Simon
15 are a result of learning some hard lessons from my relationship with him, and I certainly didn't
16 appreciate these things about Simon back then. While I was in law school, I viewed Simon and his
17 affairs as just a fact of life, and while I had some sympathy for the women who got involved with
18 him, they were adults and they knew his reputation, so what happened to them seemed to be
19 something they should have suspected.
20
21   For me, with the exception of the mild flirtations and the unwanted but relatively innocuous
22 touching, Simon Clark was a hero. He was one of the best lawyers in the firm, especially for his age.
23 During the time I was in law school Simon was in his late thirties and early forties. I saw him
24 examine witnesses and he was a master. His legal mind was brilliant. He always was able to make
25 me understand the most complicated of concepts as if they were obvious. He also took the time to
26 congratulate me on my successes in law school and to give me a "well done" on the work I did for
27 him. And although this now seems so inconsistent with his treatment of women, he was one of the
28 most active volunteer lawyers in the firm who did pro-bono work for the ACLU. To say that I
29 admired him is an understatement. I considered him to be a role model and as my mentor. After all,
30 it was Simon who encouraged me to go to law school, and, in fact, it was Simon and Cliff Fuller,
31 for whom I did quite a bit of work, who are most responsible for my becoming an associate with
32 P & G.
33
34   No one who worked as a law clerk during the school year, and no one who was a graduate
35 of the evening division of Nita University School of Law, had, as of 1994, ever been offered a
36 position as an associate at P & G. There were people in the firm, like Cliff Fuller, who were
37 graduates of Nita University, but no one from the evening division. Virtually all of the associates
38 came through the Summer Associates program, wherein approximately twenty to twenty-five of the
39 best and brightest students from around the country, and from the "best" law schools are brought in
40 for ten weeks during the summer between their second and third year of law school. Thus, I was
41 surprised when Simon Clark and Cliff Fuller came by my office one day, early in the fall of my
42 fourth year of law school, and invited me to lunch to "talk about my future with the firm." At the
43 time, Cliff was a relatively new partner (but generally considered a rising star and the protege of
44 Simon Clark) and a very active member of the hiring committee. Simon was the chair of the hiring
45 committee.
46

1   At lunch, they said that they had noted that I had not applied for an associate's position, and
2   asked why. I told them that the reason should be obvious: that the firm had never hired a law clerk
3   and never hired someone from the evening division of the Nita Law School, so that it seemed
4   pointless to do so. They both said that they had both been very impressed with my work, that it was
5   the equivalent of any of the summer associates, and that while it wasn't a foregone conclusion that
6   I would be hired, they thought I should apply and that they would both enthusiastically support my
7   application. To say that I was flattered would be an understatement. I had always harbored a fantasy
8   that I'd somehow get to be a lawyer at P & G, but I never expected it could happen.
9
10   Simon and Cliff asked where else I had applied and I told them the names of the firms.
11   Because, at the time, there was still some bias against evening-division graduates in some of the
12   largest firms (including P & G), I had applied to what was generally considered the second tier of
13   firms in the city. They were very good law firms, but did not have the size or the clout of the top
14   firms like P & G. I nonetheless followed through on my interviews with those firms, and given P &
15   G's interest, even applied to some of the other large firms in the city, several of which offered me
16   interviews.
17
18   I, of course, followed through on Simon and Cliff's suggestion and applied to P & G.
19   Although I was nervous, I must have had a good preliminary interview, because I was invited to an
20   interview with the entire hiring committee. That interview seemed to go even better. The only
21   partner who seemed negative towards me was one of the few women partners in the firm, Jayne Post.
22   Jayne was a relatively new partner at the time, and she was trying to set up a permanent domestic
23   relations section within the firm. At that point she was the only partner doing that work almost
24   exclusively and she had three associates, two of whom were women and one an African-American
25   man, working for her.
26
27   I had told the committee that I was most interested in a commercial litigation practice, but
28   that I needed to be assigned to work on cases that were primarily based in Nita City. Ms. Post
29   seemed quite negative in response to my statement that it would be necessary for me to be assigned
30   to work on Nita-based cases (as opposed to being sent across country for months at a time), because
31   of my children. At that point David was twelve and Maureen was ten (going on thirty-five) and they
32   needed a lot of my attention. Ms. Post seemed to suggest that it was inappropriate for me to ask for
33   special consideration in assignments, and although it might have been, it would have been pointless
34   for me to take a job that would take me away from my kids for an extended period of time, because
35   that would have been impossible. I wanted to be upfront about what I needed in terms of job
36   flexibility. Prior to my interviews, I didn't know how the committee would react, so I had run my
37   problem by Cliff Fuller. Cliff later told me that he had talked it over with Simon Clark and that
38   Simon didn't see a problem. After all, the firm had always accommodated me in my work as a
39   paralegal, and eventually the kids would be out on their own.
40
41   As it turned out, P & G was the most receptive to my particular needs of all the law firms
42   from whom I received offers, Jayne Post notwithstanding. Even though I received offers from five
43   other firms, including one other silk-stocking firm, I ended up going with P & G, partially because
44   of their flexibility, but mostly because I considered their offer an honor. On the day I accepted P &
45   G's offer, Simon Clark came by my office. Although I thought it was a little inappropriate, he gave
46   me a big hug and welcomed me aboard. He made me a little uncomfortable, but I was so happy to
47   be hired by P & G, and because he had helped me to get the position, I just thanked Simon for all

1   the help he had given me. He told me that he'd be sure to ask for me on some of his cases so that we
2   could work closely together. To be honest, I was flattered.
3
4   I finished out the year as a law clerk and graduated in 1994 from law school, and received
5   a number of academic awards and prizes at graduation. I am providing you with a copy of my
6   resume which contains those awards. I graduated magna cum laude, and was ranked first in the
7   evening division class. (SEE EXHIBIT 1)
8
9   I received my official letter of appointment from P & G in July of 1994. (SEE EXHIBIT 2)
10   It contained some general language about my job duties that caused me some pause in that there was
11   no mention of my understanding that I would not be assigned to cases that would take me out of Nita
12   City for extended periods of time. I mentioned this to Simon Clark and he told me not to be
13   concerned, that the letter was just a form letter and that the firm understood my need to be near my
14   children.
15
16   After taking the bar exam, I started work as an associate at P & G in September of 1994. I
17   was assigned to the litigation section as I had requested, and started off in the library with the rest
18   of my colleagues in my associates class. My beginning salary was $85,000. Partially because of my
19   years of experience as both a paralegal and a law clerk, and partially because, as I now realize, I have
20   some talent, I seemed to progress a little faster than some of the other associates in my class. It also
21   helped, I think, that I was older and had gone to law school while working full time and having the
22   responsibility of being a single parent. Because I had some maturity, the stress of the job had less
23   effect on me than it did on the typical first-year associate.
24
25   To be honest, my workload at P & G as an associate, seemed less than my workload as a law
26   clerk and a law student. In addition, because I was comfortable with the working environment at P
27   & G, and knew all the little administrative things that you need to know to survive, I spent a lot less
28   time spinning my wheels. In addition, the concept of keeping time, which was new for most of my
29   colleagues, most of whom were fresh from law school and twenty-five years old, was common to
30   me and also presented no obstacle to my doing my best work.
31
32   I was assigned to work on a wide variety of commercial litigation matters and worked with
33   a number of partners. I did very little work with Simon Clark during the first five years of my time
34   at P & G. I did an occasional memo, but I never worked a complete case from start to finish with
35   him. That may have been just happenstance, but it may also have been because of my desire to not
36   become involved in cases that involved a lot of travel for extended periods. P & G has a national
37   practice and Simon was considered to be the best litigator and trial lawyer in the firm, so he was
38   always handling the most important commercial litigation cases for the firm. When those cases were
39   in litigation, he and his litigation team would spend months at a time in the part of the country where
40   the case took place interviewing and deposing witnesses, orchestrating other discovery and making
41   and responding to motions. If the case went to trial, no matter where the trial, Simon was likely to
42   be the lead trial lawyer. As a result, he was frequently out of the office for extended periods of time,
43   so the opportunities to work for him were limited.
44
45   When I did work for Simon, our working relationship was good, and except for an occasional
46   comment about how I looked, he was very professional. In fact, the rumors about Simon and his law
47   firm romances were less frequent. Not that I sought out such rumors, but they seemed less frequent

1 and I don't know of any particular affair he had during the period of 1994 through 2000. I know that
2 Simon's son was almost killed in a car accident during that period, and maybe that caused him to
3 focus on his family life, I don't know. Whenever I was assigned to one of Simon's cases, he was
4 always complimentary of my work.
5
6   The partner I did the most work for at P & G during the period of 1994 through 1999 was
7 Cliff Fuller. In the beginning Cliff requested that I work with him on some of his smaller commercial
8 litigation cases. While some of my fellow associates preferred the big cases because there was more
9 importance attached to them in the firm, I was interested in getting some work on cases where I
10 could actually get experience doing something other than research and writing. By working with
11 Cliff on relatively smaller cases in terms of amounts involved, where there were fewer associates
12 assigned, I got a fuller look at the litigation of a case because I was involved in virtually all aspects
13 of the case. In addition, I developed an excellent working relationship with Cliff, and because he had
14 confidence in my abilities, he allowed me to take more responsibility in litigation than many of my
15 colleagues in my associates class were getting in their cases. Cliff made sure I got experience in
16 taking and defending depositions as well as motion practice, including oral arguments.
17
18   Cliff also made certain that I did work on some of the more prestigious matters in the law
19 firm, for political purposes. He counseled me that it was necessary for an associate to become known
20 for doing good work, on big cases, to progress in the firm. In terms of firm politics, big cases for big
21 clients had the most currency, and so a job well done in one of those cases did much more for your
22 reputation in the firm than an equally good job on a lesser case (involving less money or for a less
23 important client). This is the sort of thing that, but for the guidance of Cliff Fuller, I never would
24 have appreciated.
25
26   Cliff also counseled me to avoid getting involved in the domestic relations cases that were
27 handled by Jayne Post and her sub-group within the litigation section. Ms. Post had actually built
28 a rather thriving domestic relations practice within the firm. By 1999, she had two other partners and
29 four associates who worked primarily with her in her cases. From time to time she would need some
30 extra help taking depositions or writing trial memoranda and would ask for volunteers among the
31 associates to help out. Because I was marginally interested in the work and because Ms. Post was
32 one of only two women partners in the litigation section during my early years with the firm, I did
33 volunteer from time to time to do some work for her. She was very demanding, but I found her
34 comments on my performance fair and helpful. Cliff warned me that my stock in the firm would be
35 lessened if I became too identified with that kind of practice. Because he was such a good friend and
36 mentor, I followed his advice, and never did a major assignment for her. On one occasion, in 2000,
37 Ms. Post asked for me to do some work on one of her complicated divorce cases, involving the
38 equitable distribution of a number of businesses, but because I was extremely busy on another case
39 that was getting ready for trial, I was unable to accept the assignment and it was given to another
40 associate. I know that Ms. Post was offended by my not taking on the assignment, but it was really
41 out of my control.
42
43   During the period of 1994 through 1998, as in every year at P & G, my job performance was
44 evaluated. As I understood the process, the chair and the deputy chair of the litigation section
45 solicited comments from all those partners for whom I worked during the year. During that period
46 of time the chair of the litigation section was Charles Milton and his deputy was Ted Potter, both of
47 whom I had worked for on their cases over the years. I then had a meeting with them, which was

1 held close in time to my anniversary date with the firm, which in my case was September, wherein
2 they reviewed my progress with the firm. During that meeting I was given a grade. The scale was
3 A to F. After I was given my grade, I was given what I assumed was a compilation of the comments
4 that were made about me, and told how the firm would like to see me improve in the upcoming year.
5 These comments appeared to be coming from a file with my name on it. You have shown me some
6 memoranda that refer to my evaluations, and although I have no way of remembering if they track
7 what was said to me in my evaluations, they certainly could. They are accurate concerning my
8 billable hours for each year. (SEE EXHIBITS 3A–3G) I was also told how many other associates
9 in my law school class received the same grade as me, or higher. I was then told what my raise
10 would be for the next year. The raise was pegged to the grade you received. An A got you a 7
11 percent raise, a B got 5 percent, a C got 3 percent. I don't know if there was any raise associated with
12 a D because I never got one. I was never given anything in writing during any of my evaluations
13 except that I received a written confirmation of my raise. (SEE EXHIBITS 4A–4F).
14
15   In my first evaluation, in 1995, I was given the grade of C and was told that there were two
16 people in my class of twenty associates who received the grade of B and eight who received the
17 grade of C. The remainder received D grades. Although I was warned that the normal grade for an
18 associate in the first year was a C or D, because I never had received a grade in school lower than
19 a B I was a little taken aback. I was told that the partners for whom I worked were generally happy
20 with my work, but that I needed to work on being more concise in my writing style. I was also told
21 that my billable hours were okay, but that there were others who were billing more hours. I was later
22 approached by Cliff Fuller, who assured me that my work was just fine, and that I should just keep
23 plugging and that I would be all right.
24
25   I was determined in my next evaluation to improve, and I did. In 1996 through 1998, I was
26 graded as a B. In 1996, there were three other associates in my class with the grade of B, in 1997,
27 three other B's, and in 1998, four other associates were graded as high as a B. There were no A's
28 given any of the associates in our class in the litigation section during our first four years, but as I
29 understand it, that was not unusual. I guess they just wanted to keep us working. There must have
30 been some low grades however, because by 1998, our class of associates was dwindling. Of the
31 twenty people who started with my class, there were eleven remaining in 1998. Most people had
32 gone on to other firms, either within Nita City or in other states. One person, Gary Sherman, who
33 was considered one of the brightest and most talented associates in our class, took a teaching
34 position at the University of Conwell Law School in the northwest part of the state. And two people
35 who were interested in getting some actual courtroom trial experience had gone to the U.S.
36 Attorney's office in Nita City.
37
38   Each of the oral evaluations in 1996 through 1998, were, for the most part, complimentary.
39 There seemed to be a consensus that my research and writing skills were quite good, and really
40 needed no improvement. Apparently there was one partner in each of these evaluations who
41 questioned my analytical skills, but I was not given any specific examples of where my analytical
42 skills were lacking. I was told by Cliff Fuller not to worry about that particular comment, because
43 it was from a partner who thought that because I was an evening division graduate that I could not
44 be as smart as the other associates. Cliff said that although this opinion was unfair, that I should just
45 ignore it and he confided in me that when he was an associate that he got similar comments, just
46 because he was the first University of Nita law school graduate to join P & G. I don't know if Cliff

1   was telling me the truth about his receiving bad evaluations, but given his reputation in the firm as
2   one of the best and the brightest, he sure made me feel better.
3
4   Another negative comment that I received in one evaluation, I think it was in 1998, was that
5   because I was unavailable to travel on cases for extended periods of time, due to my child care
6   responsibilities, that I was somehow not fulfilling my obligations to the firm. I remember talking
7   with Rachel Levin, a friend from my paralegal days, and Milton's secretary about the comment and
8   she encouraged me to talk to Milton about it. She said he was fair. I reminded Charles Milton and
9   Ted Potter that I had made clear when I was hired that my travel was limited, and that the firm had
10 hired me nonetheless, and that I therefore thought the comment was unfair.
11
12 Q: Did you ever talk to Milton about that issue again?
13
14 A: Yes, I was later called back into Charles Milton's office, and it was explained to me that the
15   comment about not traveling had been made by a woman partner who felt that my children
16   were old enough to be left with a child-care provider in the home if I needed to be out of
17   town for an extended period of time.
18
19 Q: What was your reaction to what Milton had to say?
20
21 A: I think that somehow they thought that because the comment was made by a woman, that it
22   was fair.
23
24 Q: What did you say to Milton?
25
26 A: I again stated that I had come to the firm with an understanding that my travel would be
27   limited.
28
29 Q: How did he respond?
30
31 A: He didn't really. With that, the conversation was terminated.
32
33 Q: Just like that?
34
35 A: He wasn't rude or anything, but he got a phone call and told me that he had to take the call
36   and asked that I excuse him, so I left the office.
37
38 Q: Was anything else said to you by Milton about the issue of your traveling on firm business?
39
40 A: No, it never came up again with him.
41
42   The only women partners in the litigation section at the time I worked at the firm were Jayne
43 Post, Sherry Barker, and Ann Feinman who worked in the domestic relations unit and Cheryl Stein
44 who worked primarily in bankruptcy litigation. Because I had not worked for anyone other that Ms.
45 Post, I assume that the comment came from her, even though I never was asked to do any extended
46 travel by her. As I said, I rarely did any work for her at all.
47

1   The only other negative comment that I received in my first four evaluations was that "I was
2   not aggressive enough" and that I lacked "toughness." When I asked for specific examples, none
3   were forthcoming, but it was a consistent comment. I spoke with Cliff Fuller about those comments
4   as well. I remember specifically having a conversation with him after my 1998 evaluation, and he
5   said that the "lack of aggressiveness" was a common comment made about women associates by
6   older male partners and that I shouldn't be overly concerned about it. He said that the times were
7   changing, but slowly, and the fact that Cheryl Stein had made partner in the litigation section in 1997
8   to work in the bankruptcy sub-group was a good sign for my future. He also pointed out that it looked
9   like women in both the tax and corporate sections would be made partner in that year.
10
11   · My fifth year at the firm was a particularly difficult one for me. In the fall of 1998 my father
12 was diagnosed as having pancreatic cancer. He only lived for two months after being diagnosed (he
13 died in November of 1998) and I spent a lot of time traveling from Nita City back home to
14 Connecticut. The travel, plus the emotional upheaval, affected my work, both in terms of quantity
15 and quality. Cliff Fuller, who by that time was the deputy chair of the litigation section (Simon Clark
16 was the chair), approached me with some complaints. When I told him what I was going through,
17 he was sympathetic, but told me to use my work as a refuge so that I didn't adversely affect my
18 future with the firm.
19
20   That year was also the year that David was a junior in high school and Maureen was a
21 freshman. David got involved with a bad group of kids. His grades in the first and second quarter
22 were well below normal; he was a solid B+/A student and his grades were in the C range for those
23 quarters. Eventually, I caught him with some marijuana in his room. We spent a lot of time working
24 through that problem and he seemed to respond pretty well, and by the third quarter his grades were
25 into the B+ range and by the end of his junior year he was back on track with good grades.
26
27   Maureen went through the classic teenage problems that all young girls face during that first
28 year of high school. It was especially difficult for us, because there was no father there to help her
29 through that time when teenage girls want nothing to do with their mothers. Nonetheless we
30 weathered the storm and by the summer of 1999, we were once again a functioning family.
31
32   The effect of all of this was that my billable hours were down for that year and the quality
33 of my work also suffered. Even Cliff Fuller was less than complimentary about my work. I was
34 trying hard, but with my personal problems, I was just not functioning at anywhere near my normal
35 level.
36
37   My firm evaluation for that year reflected the kind of year I had. The evaluation was held in
38 Simon Clark's office. Simon had been made the chair of the litigation section of the firm in the fall
39 of 1999. Cliff Fuller was also there as the deputy chair. Simon told me that although he and Cliff had
40 fought very hard for me, and had asked that my personal problems be considered, that my grade for
41 my fifth year was a C. They said that there was one associate who received an A and two associates
42 who received B's and three other associates who received C's. They told me that my hours were not
43 acceptable and that for the first time, they had received some substantial complaints about the quality
44 of my work. They both said that they believed that I was partnership material and that I had what it
45 took to make partner, but that my C grade was a real problem.
46

1	Simon told me that I had basically three ways to go. First, I could look for a job with another
2	firm, and that the firm would be very complimentary of me in giving recommendations. One of the
3	associates who received a C took this option. Second, he could arrange for a very good position for
4	me in the general counsel's office of Nita Computer World, which was one of the firm's best
5	corporate clients. He said that two other associates who were graded at C had chosen to take the
6	option of going to work with a client company, but that the Nita Computer World job was the best
7	such position available. Third, I could come to work with him on a major piece of antitrust litigation
8	that was just gearing up on behalf of Nita Computer World, work like hell, and repair my reputation
9	within the firm.
10	
11	To me, there was no choice. I chose to go to work on the Nita Computer World (NCW)
12	litigation with Simon Clark. I was not a quitter and I had worked too hard to leave P & G under a
13	cloud. I knew that many other former associates with P & G had gone to work for the firm's clients
14	and that the jobs had great security and benefits, but I wasn't willing, at that time in my life, to settle
15	for such a job. Simon said that he knew that I would choose the third option, but made it clear that
16	my career with P & G was on the line and that he expected my best work on the case. There were
17	two young partners assigned to the case and four other associates. I was the senior associate on the
18	NCW case.
19	
20	The work on the NCW case was the most challenging and rewarding legal work I had ever
21	done. I use many of the things I learned during that litigation in the teaching of my complex
22	litigation seminar at the law school. The case, which involved an allegation of price fixing on the
23	part of NCW and other distributors of computer hardware and software, was complicated and
24	presented fascinating legal and tactical issues. Simon was right, though. The hours were long and
25	exhausting, and because so much was on the line, both for me personally, and for the client, I worked
26	harder than I had ever worked before. This was especially so because the judge set a very quick
27	discovery deadline of six months, and set the case for a firm trial date in June of 2000.
28	
29	Because I was the senior associate on the case, I helped prepare the partners for depositions,
30	drafted all motions and supporting memoranda for use by the partners (who made any necessary
31	additions or corrections), and was allowed to conduct some of the peripheral depositions myself. I
32	was involved in all aspects of case planning and litigation strategy. The NCW case only increased
33	my admiration for Simon Clark as a lawyer. His insights were incredible, his instincts sharp and his
34	ability to get information, both through document production and depositions was nothing short of
35	brilliant in my opinion.
36	
37	As I said, I was involved in all aspects of the litigation. I often times traveled with Simon or
38	one of the other partners for depositions both in and out of the state. The travel wasn't all that
39	frequent and usually did not involve more than two or three days away from home in a row, so I
40	agreed to the travel. Even though I was a little nervous about leaving the kids, David was being very
41	responsible, having received an early acceptance into the honors program and a partial academic
42	scholarship at Nita University, and Maureen, after her bad year, seemed to be doing very well both
43	academically and otherwise. In addition, I knew that my career was on the line, so the travel, even
44	though not optimal, was necessary.
45	
46	It was on one of these trips out of town, in January of 2000, that Simon Clark made his first
47	sexual proposition to me. After a particularly grueling day of depositions and a long preparation

22

Polisi Case File

1   session in his room, Simon ordered up a late night meal with some wine and we sat and relaxed. Talk
2   turned to our personal lives. Simon asked about the kids and I told him they were doing well. He
3   then asked how I was doing. I told him how happy I was working on the NCW case, and he said that
4   my work was first-rate and that my prospects for partnership were looking better every day. He then
5   asked about my social life, and although it was none of his business, I told him that between the job
6   and the kids, I had no social life. Simon then started talking about his marriage and his kids. He said
7   that he and his wife were married only in name, and that they only stayed married for his children,
8   the youngest of whom was a high school senior.
9
10   Although I was uncomfortable with the conversation, I was exhausted from work, and the
11 closeness of our working relationship made the conversation come pretty easily. Simon then made
12 some comment about how different I was from his wife. He said that she seemed to care about
13 nothing other than her social standing and really cared little for him or their children. He said that
14 he admired me for what I had accomplished, both professionally and with my children. At some
15 point during the conversation he got up and walked around the back of my chair and started to
16 massage my shoulders. Although this made me more than a little uncomfortable, I'll have to admit
17 that it felt good, so I didn't protest. He then kissed me on the neck. Although I shouldn't have been,
18 given Simon's reputation, I was surprised and I jumped up out of my chair.
19
20   Simon seemed shocked by my reaction, but I just said that I wasn't ready for that kind of
21 relationship, and that I should probably leave. He told me that there was no need for that, that he was
22 attracted to me, but that he had misread my signals. He apologized for being so forward. I sat back
23 in the chair and we talked about the case and the next day's deposition for about a half hour. I then
24 went back to my room.
25
26   The next day Simon was very cool and formal with me. I guess I must have bruised his ego.
27 I assumed that things would get back to normal between us as the case continued at its breakneck
28 pace and after a couple of more days of the silent treatment, our working relationship was back to
29 normal. In March, we were out of town on another set of depositions, and again were meeting in his
30 room after a day of depositions. After we finished our business, Simon asked if I was interested in
31 a little relaxation and conversation. When I hesitated, he said something like "just conversation," and
32 I relaxed and agreed to share a late supper and a glass of wine with him.
33
34   Simon was particularly talkative, and after inquiring after my family and me, he started to
35 talk about his relationship with his family. He again complained about his wife having more concern
36 for her country club and social gatherings than him and his children. He told me that his marriage
37 that had lasted over twenty-five years had been nothing more than a shell for the last fifteen. He
38 asked me if I was aware of the rumors about him and other women and I admitted that I was. He
39 didn't deny them, but explained them away as his searching for something better. He then told me
40 that once his son graduated from high school that June, that he was going to file for divorce. He said
41 that he had thought about divorce before, but that when he talked to his wife that she made it very
42 clear that he would have a hard time seeing the children, and that she would use his affairs to ensure
43 that his access to the children was severely limited. According to Simon, his relationship with his
44 children was strained at best, because of his long hours at work and long periods of time away from
45 home, and he didn't want to lose what little relationship he had with them.
46

1   He also said that when he was younger he worried about the effect a divorce would have on
2   his career, given that many of his corporate clients were controlled by social friends who were
3   originally friends of his wife and her family. He said that he now understood that although social
4   relationships may open doors, that corporate decisions are made on sound business bases, not on
5   social friendship. He was now confident, or so he said, that his clients would remain with him
6   regardless of whether he and his wife divorced, so that he was ready to go forward with the divorce.
7   In fact, he said, the only thing that kept him going was his work; that his only regret was that he
8   didn't have someone special to share it with.
9
10   To be honest, I was moved by what Simon had to say. He seemed so sad about his life, which
11   from my perspective seemed so glamorous. I really wanted to hug him, but what had happened
12   before between us stopped me, I guess. I told him that I was sure that everything would work out for
13   him, that I hoped it would. He smiled at me in sort of a sad way, and said he hoped so too. And that
14   was that. He then changed the topic of the conversation back to the NCW case.
15
16   That night was the beginning of a different relationship between Simon Clark and me.
17   Although he didn't attempt anything physical, at the end of long days, both on the road and in Nita
18   City, we would often have long talks about the most personal of things. We were not intimate
19   sexually, but we were intimate. He told me all about himself and his life and I did likewise. We spent
20   an enormous amount of time together through the conclusion of the NCW case which was in early
21   June of 2000, when the case settled on very favorable terms for our client. The case was also a
22   personal success. I was uniformly praised for my work on the case, in particular for my work on a
23   protective order concerning some trade secrets of NCW's that was eventually granted by the court.
24   I received a copy of a letter from the Vice President and General Counsel of NCW to Simon that
25   acknowledged my contributions to the case. (SEE EXHIBIT 6)
26
27   NCW was so pleased with the outcome that they gave the members of the litigation team a
28   trip, with spouses, for a week in the Bahamas. Everyone on the team including all the lawyers and
29   the three paralegals were invited. Because I wasn't married and because Simon apparently never
30   went anywhere with his wife, we were the only people there without a significant other. On our third
31   night there, one thing led to another and Simon and I ended up sleeping together. I should have
32   known that it was the wrong thing to do, but it happened anyway. We spent a terrific week together
33   and Simon started talking about our future together.
34
35   I know that sometime during the week I asked Simon about when his son was going to
36   graduate from high school and he told me that the boy needed to attend summer school in order to
37   finish his degree and that he had pulled some strings to get him into college. Simon then volunteered
38   that as soon as his boy was firmly in school that he was going to file for divorce. I know I should
39   have recognized that he was repeating the pattern I heard he had with other women but I wanted our
40   relationship to work. It was, after all, the only other serious relationship I had with a man other than
41   my husband. I rationalized that this time Simon was really different for a number of reasons. First,
42   unlike his other conquests I was not young. At that time I was in my late thirties and the other
43   women were all in their twenties. Second, the way our relationship came about seemed so natural
44   that I was sure he was sincere. Third, the rumors about Simon had lessened in recent years and I
45   guess I wanted to believe that he had changed. Finally, the last kid being out of the house, seemed
46   like a good time to end a bad relationship, and from everything he said he truly had a bad
47   relationship with his wife.

1   The rest of that summer flew by. I was extremely happy with both my job and my personal
2   life. My kids were doing great. They had met Simon and they seemed to like him. I didn't think that
3   they knew what my relationship with him was, but as it turned out, they knew exactly what was
4   going on. I told Simon that in light of my personal relationship with him, that I thought that I
5   shouldn't work with him unless he absolutely needed me and he agreed. That summer I got terrific
6   assignments, better than ever before. The cases were interesting and I was asked to work on
7   interesting issues. My relationship with Simon was also terrific. We spent time away from the office
8   together, including some weekend getaways. The only problem I had was on Labor Day weekend
9   when he said that he had to spend it with his wife's family at some gathering in Martha's Vineyard.
10 Simon told me that he really didn't want to go, but that it was the last chance he had to be with his
11 son before he went off to school and that his other kids would also be there, including his oldest
12 daughter who had just had her first child, a son. So even though I wasn't happy about it, I didn't put
13 up a fuss about his going. I spent the weekend with my kids, and as it turned out we had a wonderful
14 time.
15
16   I had my sixth-year evaluation right after Labor Day in 2000. It was again held in Simon's
17 office and Cliff Fuller was also there. I was thrilled when Simon told me that my grade for the year
18 was an A. He said that the partners in the litigation section were very impressed with all the terrific
19 work I did on the NCW case and with the enormous number of hours I billed for the year. I was also
20 told that the management people at NCW were pleased with my work and that they would be pleased
21 to have me work on other cases for them, which was consistent with the letter I had seen from NCW
22 to Simon. (SEE EXHIBIT 6) Finally they told me that in my class, only one other person was graded
23 at the A level, and that it looked very good for me for a positive partnership vote in the spring of
24 2001. I was on cloud nine. Simon came out of his chair and gave me a big hug and a kiss. Because
25 Cliff was in the room I was a little embarrassed, but at the time, nothing could have upset me. I do
26 remember telling Simon that in the future we should not have any public displays of affection in the
27 office, that I thought it was unprofessional and that others might hold it against me. Simon agreed
28 with me, but said that at some point that the people in the firm would have to get used to it.
29
30   In fact, the day after my evaluation Cliff Fuller came to my office and asked if I minded a
31 little advice from an old friend. I, of course, was interested in what he had to say. Cliff asked if I was
32 aware of Simon's sexual history with women in the firm. I told him that I was, but that Simon had
33 told me that once his son was away at college that he was going to leave his wife. When Cliff started
34 to say something like, "he's said that before" I told him that I didn't want to talk about my
35 relationship with Simon. Cliff backed off, but did say that he hoped things worked out for me, but
36 if they didn't he wasn't sure that he could protect me at the firm. His statement sort of shook me, but
37 I didn't respond. I felt that I had weathered the storm at the firm by way of long hours and hard
38 work, and that was all the protection I needed. I'll have to admit that what Cliff said was unsettling
39 and made me feel somewhat vulnerable, but I certainly didn't realize how vulnerable I turned out
40 to be.
41
42   In September of 2000 I started work on another case for NCW. It wasn't of the same size in
43 dollar terms or complexity, but it was nonetheless interesting. Cliff Fuller was the partner in charge
44 of the case, although Simon retained some supervisory control over all of NCW's litigation. As a
45 result, when I had to travel to some of NCW's offices out of state, Simon, who was not involved in
46 any special case at the time, sometimes came along. It was on one of these trips in late September
47 or early October, that I had a conversation with Simon about his marital status. When I asked

1   whether he had seen a lawyer about his divorce, his first response was to get angry and snapped out
2   something like "the marriage lasted over twenty-five years, it takes some time to end it," but then
3   he calmed down almost immediately and said that it was important for his son to be into his school
4   routine before hitting him with that kind of news. He said that he wanted to give him a semester to
5   get adjusted. I appreciated that his son had some academic problems in high school, and that college
6   took some adjustment so I just accepted Simon's explanation.
7
8   I then got heavily involved in the NCW case and was working fairly hard on it with Cliff.
9   Cliff never asked directly about my relationship with Simon, but every once in a while he asked how
10   things were going for me. Even though by late fall I was having more questions about whether
11   Simon would ever leave his wife, I never said anything about it to Cliff.
12
13   As it turned out, the Christmas holidays spelled the end of my relationship with Simon Clark.
14   We got into a fight in early December about where Simon was going to spend Christmas day. He
15   wanted to spend Christmas and the week after Christmas on a vacation with his family, including
16   his wife, his children, and their families at his home in Palm Beach, Florida. He told me it was one
17   of the only times when he got to see kids and even though he preferred to be with me, that he thought
18   he should spend one last holiday with his family before his divorce. I was very unhappy about his
19   holiday plans, but Simon promised me that at the end of the vacation, he would spend an extra day
20   in Florida with his wife, and tell her that he was getting a divorce. This made me feel better, but of
21   course he never did ask for the divorce.
22
23   Simon returned to Nita City right after the first of the year and came over to my house to see
24   me. Fortunately my kids were out, because when I asked him how his wife took the divorce news,
25   Simon told me that he hadn't said anything to her about the divorce. I got very angry and started
26   screaming at him. He tried to calm me down and eventually did, and told me that he was still going
27   to ask for the divorce, but that his son was having a rough time adjusting to school and that he
28   wanted to wait until the boy had finished his freshman year before subjecting him to the upheaval
29   of a divorce. I wanted to believe Simon, but I was still very angry. I told him to leave, which he did.
30
31   Over the next week, Simon was out of town on business. He called a number of times and
32   sent flowers, but I didn't return his calls. I spent most of the week trying to figure out what I was
33   going to do and came to the conclusion that even though I wanted him to, that Simon was probably
34   never going to leave his wife. I decided to give him one last chance. When he returned to Nita City
35   I invited him to my house for dinner. This would have been around January 15. I told him how I felt
36   and that if he loved me and wanted to be with me that he had to get a lawyer and get divorce
37   proceedings started in one week. He started to protest about his son, and I told him that I didn't want
38   to hear about his son, that it was time for Simon to decide what he really wanted. I then sent him
39   home and told him to call me with his decision.
40
41   The next week went by extremely slowly. The stress must have shown on me because a
42   number of people asked me if I was well. That weekend Simon came to my house. He asked if I
43   wanted to go away with him for a vacation in the Bahamas and pulled out some plane tickets from
44   his pocket. I assumed he had told his wife he wanted a divorce, so I ran to hug him. I then asked him
45   how she took the news and Simon told me to take it easy, but that it hadn't happened yet. I pushed
46   him away and asked him to leave. He tried to grab me but when I insisted he just got angry. I'll never

1 forget the anger on his face as he turned to walk out the door. As he left he said, "You're all the
2 same. You don't realize when you've got a good thing going. You'll regret this, I promise you."
3
4   That's the last conversation I had with Simon Clark for about two months. He went off to
5 try a case in Seattle. He never wrote or called. Apparently our break-up didn't affect him much
6 because he won the case. When he returned to Nita City he did call to ask me to dinner, but I refused.
7 I had spent the time he was away trying to get over Simon, and didn't want to take the chance of
8 getting involved with him again. That two months had been very hard for me. I had trouble at work
9 concentrating in the beginning, but eventually I came around and immersed myself in my work. But
10 probably because I wasn't eating particularly well, I caught a lot of colds, some of which were bad
11 enough to keep me out of work. They continued well into the spring of 2001.
12
13   Because of my health, I welcomed the fact that my assignments seemed to lighten up in the
14 winter and early spring of 2001, and I wasn't very busy. As it turned out, that was only a portent of
15 things to come. In May of 2001, Cliff Fuller asked me to come to his office.
16
17 Q: I assume you went to Mr. Fuller's office.
18
19 A: Yes I did.
20
21 Q: What did he have to say?
22
23 A: He told me that the firm was about to consider three people in my class for partnership and
24   that if I wanted, I too could be brought up.
25
26 Q: Was that it?
27
28 A;   No, he said, however, that given the drop-off in my production and the lingering problems
29   some people had with my law school background, my early refusal to travel, and my lack of
30   toughness, that it was his advice that I put off the partnership decision for another year so I
31   could improve my chances.
32
33 Q: How did you respond?
34
35 A: When I protested, he told me that he was only the messenger, that he was in my corner and
36   that I could count on his vote, but that he was fairly certain that if I pushed the matter, I
37   would be turned down.
38
39 Q: What did you say?
40
41 A: I asked Cliff whether this was Simon's doing, and he deflected my question and told me that
42   this was his best advice, but that he was willing to fight for me if that was my desire. He told
43   me to think it over for a couple of days and get back to him.
44
45   The next couple of days I went through all the options in my head. It became obvious that
46 Simon was doing to me what he apparently had done to his other former lovers. I then realized that
47 the drop off in my assignments was no accident, and that while I was feeling fortunate to have some

1   break in my assignments, that the lack of assignments was designed to hurt me. No, I didn't protest
2   the lack of work to anyone. I just viewed it as a cyclical thing. I had been very busy in the fall,
3   working on the second NCW case with Cliff and several other matters. My billables for September,
4   2000 through January, 2001 were approximately 850 hours, which on average was better than my
5   previous year. After speaking with Cliff, I checked my billables for February, 2001 through May,
6   2001 and they were only 550 hours. I'll admit that wasn't very good, but if you projected from the
7   first four months together with the second four months, to the last four months of the year, I would
8   have ended up with a respectable 2100 hours for the year. That is, I billed 1400 hours for the first
9   two-thirds of the year, which projects to 2100 hours for the entire year, assuming I got decent
10 assignments. I eventually concluded that I was better off coming up for partnership in that year,
11 while my NCW success was still fresh in everyone's mind, than waiting for a year of reduced
12 assignments and letting them drive me out that way. I gave Cliff my decision, and although he tried
13 to talk me out of it, he promised to go forward.
14
15   About a week later, Cliff came to my office and gave me the bad news. He said that I didn't
16 make it out of the litigation section with a recommendation of partnership. He said that it was close,
17 but that I had just missed. He told me that the firm was giving me six months to find another
18 position. I was obviously very upset. I asked Cliff if Simon spoke in favor of me. Cliff said that the
19 meeting was confidential and that he couldn't tell me who said what. He did say that he was sure that
20 Simon would give me a good reference if I wanted one. He then said he was sorry. I also asked Cliff
21 how the three others who were up for partnership had fared. He told me two men, Roger Kramer and
22 Mark Hancock, had made partner, and that Michael DeAngelo had decided to put off consideration
23 for partnership a year. I asked Cliff if I could come up again in the next year, and he told me that
24 once an associate chose to go forward, as I did, there was no turning back. He also said that he
25 doubted that a new vote would make any difference.
26
27   I was hurt and angry over my treatment by P & G and was convinced that the cause of my
28 being denied a partnership was because of my dumping Simon Clark. I therefore went to the Nita
29 office of the Equal Employment Opportunity Commission to file a complaint. After some research,
30 I learned that complaining to the EEOC was a necessary prerequisite to bringing suit against P & G.
31 The interviewer seemed sympathetic, but said that it was unlikely that she would get to my claim
32 for a long while. She told me to contact her in 180 days so that she could issue a "Right to Sue" letter
33 if I wanted to pursue my claim in the courts. I did so, and received a form giving me the right to sue
34 in December of 2001, shortly after I resigned from P & G.
35
36   I took some time off from work to sort through my career options. During this period, I
37 quietly looked into some other associate positions, but nothing really caught my fancy, and although
38 I sent out some resumes, nothing came of it. Several firms seemed to be interested initially and had
39 me send reference letters, but only a couple of firms gave me what I would consider a full interview,
40 and no job offer was made. Because I didn't have the ability to bring any business to a new firm at
41 that time, my prospects in Nita City to be a partner in a large firm didn't seem great. What did
42 surprise me, was that I didn't even receive any permanent associate offers. I thought too about
43 moving to another city, but Nita had been my home and I really didn't want to leave.
44
45   One night as I was absent mindedly going through the mail, I saw an alumni newsletter from
46 the law school and I started to think about teaching as a career. The next day I called Gary Sherman,
47 who was in my associates class at P & G and who had left for a teaching career several years before.

1   He was very helpful and enthusiastic about my trying to find a teaching job. He advised me that the
2   best thing I could do was to work some interesting project from my practice into a law review article
3   and attempt to get published before the law school hiring convention in the fall of 2001.
4
5   The more I thought of it, the more teaching appealed to me. During my law school years I
6   had enjoyed the research and writing experience that I had with the Law Review, and I remember
7   harboring some thoughts about a teaching career sometime in the future when my kids were grown
8   and I only had myself to look after. In practice, you never get to finish looking into some of the
9   interesting legal and intellectual issues that arise beyond what is necessary to deal with a client's
10   problems and that was always somewhat frustrating to me. In addition, although my kids were still
11   in school, and the money that you can make in practice was still important, I had never acquired a
12   life style that demanded a huge salary so even though I realized that I would have to take a
13   substantial pay cut, I thought that I should explore the teaching option. It was early in my career for
14   such a move, but I thought that exploration of the teaching option was worth the effort.
15
16   I went back to the firm the next week and started to look back over my files for some of the
17   issues that had intrigued me when I was working on them, but never got finished, at least to my
18   satisfaction. When I was working on a case, I would often make some notes about how I would like
19   to explore a particular issue in the future if time allowed. Within a week I identified two particularly
20   interesting issues and started looking into them. I ended up writing on the tension between the law
21   of privilege and work product, when such material is used by a client for the purposes of refreshing
22   recollection, and the right of opposing counsel to see such material. Given that I was assigned very
23   little work, there was little to distract me from my scholarly work, and by the early fall, I had an
24   article to be submitted for publication. Working on the article was one of the most satisfying
25   intellectual experiences of my career and confirmed that I should continue to explore a position in
26   legal education. I was lucky in that an article that had been promised for a symposium issue on
27   current issues in litigation in the Nita University Law Review did not materialize and my article was
28   accepted to fill that void.
29
30   I spent the rest of the fall working on another article between the sporadic assignments I
31   received from the firm, and this piece on conflicts of interest in antitrust litigation was in rough draft
32   form by the time of the Association of American Law Schools hiring convention. I got about ten
33   initial interviews and was invited to four on-campus interviews in December of 2001. As a result of
34   the interviewing process I received an offer from Conwell University School of Law. Fortunately
35   for me, the offer did not come through until the later spring of 2002. At the same time, I was
36   working as an Adjunct Professor at my alma mater, filling in for Professor Levinson, who was
37   visiting at another law school. When Professor Levinson decided to stay at that school, I received
38   an offer from Nita University to join the faculty as an Associate Professor in the fall of 2002. I am
39   told that the offer was based in part on strong reports on my teaching from the students in my spring
40   2002 classes. Because Nita City is my home, I chose to take the offer from Nita University, even
41   though I'm sure I would have enjoyed working with Gary Sherman at Conwell Law School. My
42   starting salary at the Law School was $75,000.
43
44   The law school offers came at a good time for me because I needed an ego boost and two
45   teaching offers in a tough market restored some of the self-esteem I lost in my unsuccessful search
46   for practice jobs in Nita City. As I said, I had applied to a number of law firms, beginning in the
47   summer of 2001, but no positions came open for me. I had a number of interviews, but received no

1　offers. Initially, I thought that the whole experience at P & G had demoralized me, and that I was
2　not coming across as very confident in the interviews I had, or that my foray into academic writing
3　had steered me towards an academic career, which had some impact on my enthusiasm in law firm
4　job interviews. As it turned out, my real problem with law firm jobs was apparently Simon Clark.
5
6　　　　　Cliff Fuller told me in June of 2001 that he had written a glowing recommendation
7　concerning my abilities for Simon Clark's signature, and that I should feel free to use both him and
8　Simon as references when looking for a law firm position. Although I was hesitant to use Simon as
9　a reference, I did so after Cliff showed me a copy of the letter he drafted for Simon's signature. (SEE
10　EXHIBIT 10) I got a phone call after the first of the year in 2002 from a friend of mine at Morrison
11　& Farrow, which is a law firm in Nita City to which I had applied in June or July of 2001. This
12　friend told me that she had seen the Simon Clark recommendation letter and that it was not a good
13　one. She also told me that John Randall of her firm spoke with Simon about me, and that Simon was
14　very negative in his evaluation of my abilities. She eventually made a copy of Simon's letter from
15　their files which obviously is not a good letter of recommendation, and not consistent with my
16　performance at P & G. (SEE EXHIBIT 11) I recognize the handwriting at the bottom of the page on
17　Exhibit 11, that says to "be careful," as Simon Clark's. He obviously deep-sixed me with Morrison
18　& Farrow. I can only assume that he did the same with other firms who inquired of him, which
19　explains why I received no law firm job offers.
20
21　　　　　I stayed on at P & G until the end of my six-month grace period, just to save some more
22　money. I turned in my resignation to Cliff Fuller. Cliff has been very supportive of me in my
23　searching for positions, both in practice and academia, and although he tried to get excited about the
24　adjunct position, I could tell he was disappointed for me. He inquired about my finances and offered
25　to loan me some money if I needed it. I told him that I appreciated his concern, but that I would be
26　all right. I had cashed in my retirement account at P & G, so that more than covered me for the short
27　term when combined with my salary as an adjunct at the law school. I was also hopeful that one of
28　my law school teaching interviews would pan out into a full-time position. Apparently P & G was
29　notified by the EEOC about my complaint against them, because Cliff offered to give whatever
30　testimony he could about my time at P & G. Since my resignation from the firm, I have had dinner
31　with Cliff on a number of occasions. He has been a good friend to me. We don't often talk about P
32　& G, but Cliff did tell me late 2001 or early 2002 that he had become disenchanted with the firm and
33　firm politics.
34
35　　　　　In January of 2002, when I told Cliff what Simon had done to me when I had applied for law
36　firm jobs, he was visibly upset. He later checked and found that Simon had indeed written his own
37　reference letter which was far from complimentary to all of the firms I applied to and informed them
38　that Simon would act as a reference. It was when Cliff called me with that news that he also told me
39　that he was considering leaving the firm for a position with NCW. In the end, Cliff was appointed
40　the Vice President and General Counsel of Nita Computer World. He started with them in April of
41　2002. Shortly after beginning at NCW, Cliff and I had one of our dinners. At that time he offered
42　me a position in NCW's legal department to assist in managing the company's litigation. Although
43　I was flattered by the offer, I had just been offered the full-time position at the law school and had
44　accepted that offer. Even though the NCW job would have paid a starting salary of $90,000, and my
45　law school salary started at $75,000, I wanted to give teaching a good try. My semester as an adjunct
46　had been very challenging and rewarding, and, as I said, I was well received by my students. I also
47　liked the fact that research and writing whatever I was interested in was a job requirement.

1   Although I am very happy at the law school, I do miss the different challenges and the highs
2 and lows of practice. I worked very hard at P & G to succeed and deserved to be treated better than
3 I was. I believe that my failure to receive an offer of partnership was a direct result of my breaking
4 off my relationship with Simon Clark. I also believe that P & G discriminates against women. No
5 woman has ever been made a partner in the litigation section to perform regular commercial
6 litigation while I was there. The only women partners in litigation were either Jayne Post's domestic
7 relations group, where in addition to Jayne there are three other women partners (Sherry Barker, Ann
8 Feinman, and Georgia Bratton) and in the bankruptcy group which has only three partners, two of
9 whom are women (Cheryl Stein and Kathryn Kowalski). Of the general litigation partners, of which
10 there are thirty in the firm, there are no women.
11
12   I also believe that Simon Clark slandered me when talking to people at firms where I applied
13 for associate positions after being forced out of P & G. Although his letter (SEE EXHIBIT 11) is not
14 negative in an absolute sense, it is not a fair representation of my work at the firm, and certainly is
15 not the kind of letter on which you base a positive hiring decision. In addition, his oral statements,
16 at least to John Randall at Morrison & Farrow, (SEE EXHIBIT 18) were out-and-out false.

I have read this deposition and it is complete and accurate.

Margaret Polisi

Margaret Polisi

Subscribed and sworn before me this 10th day of December, 2002.

Harry Gibbons

Harry Gibbons
Certified Shorthand Reporter

      This deposition was taken in the office of the counsel for the defendants on November 24th, 2002. This deposition was given under oath and was read and signed by the deponent.

DEPOSITION OF CLIFFORD FULLER

1 　　　My name is Cliff Fuller. I am forty-three years old and work as the Vice President and
2 General Counsel of Nita Computer World, which is a national wholesaler and retailer of computers
3 and other electronic equipment. Until April 1st of 2002, I was a general litigation partner at the law
4 firm of Parker & Gould (P & G) in Nita City. For the period 1999 until the time that I left the firm,
5 I was the deputy chair of the litigation section of the firm. I am single, having gotten a divorce from
6 my wife, Gerry, in 1989. Fortunately, we did not have any children.
7
8 　　　I was born and raised in Nita City and graduated from the public schools. I have six siblings,
9 all but two of whom still live in the area. My brother Mike lives in Los Angeles and my sister, Carol,
10 lives in Atlanta. My parents, both of whom are still living, also live in Nita City. My father is a
11 retired postal worker. I received my undergraduate degree in Political Science from Bucknell
12 University in Lewisburg, Pennsylvania, in 1983 where I was an academic scholarship student. I
13 graduated with honors, and although I was accepted by a number of the so-called top law schools,
14 none of them offered me any substantial financial aid, so when I was accepted to the University of
15 Nita School of Law I decided to take advantage of the relatively low in-state tuition and enrolled in
16 September of 1983. I was also married in the summer of 1983 to Gerry. She was also a graduate of
17 Bucknell, which is where we met.
18
19 　　　While I was going to law school, Gerry attended the business school at Nita University. She
20 got her MBA in 1985. Gerry's job opportunities were somewhat limited by the fact that I still had
21 a year to go at law school. Although I considered transferring to another school, wherever Gerry's
22 best job opportunities took us, I was elected the editor-in-chief of the Law Review, and we thought
23 that it was important for my career that I finish up at Nita University. Gerry turned down some very
24 attractive offers elsewhere, and took a job in Nita City. As it turned out, I always felt guilty about
25 that decision, and I think that Gerry was always a little resentful. This was especially so when I
26 received an offer from P & G which was then, and I think now, considered to be one of the best firms
27 in the region. I think that Gerry felt, and I think it was fair for her to feel, that she had sacrificed in
28 her career for me, while I never had to sacrifice anything in my career for her. This resentment was
29 really the foundation of our marital problems which persisted over the years until we separated in
30 1988 and eventually divorced in 1989. Gerry now lives and works in New York City, where she is
31 a very successful investment counselor.
32
33 　　　To be honest, I was surprised that I ended up at P & G. Although I had a good record at law
34 school, graduating first in my class, P & G had the reputation of being an elitist law firm and I was
35 the first Nita law graduate to ever receive an offer from them. Even though I had offers from most
36 of the other large law firms in the city for the summer between my second and third year, I chose to
37 go to P & G to prove to them that Nita was actually a fine law school. Perhaps because of that, I
38 worked especially hard, and apparently made a good impression, because I was offered a position
39 as an associate with the firm in 1986, which I accepted. Aside from the honor of being the first Nita
40 law grad, the other reason I accepted P & G's offer was Simon Clark.
41
42 　　　During my summer at P & G I was assigned to work with Simon Clark on a fairly routine
43 contract action involving two Nita City companies. He gave me interesting work to do, and always
44 took the time to explain how what I was doing fit into the whole of the case. He also invited me

1   along on depositions and to settlement negotiations. I was allowed to sit in on planning and strategy
2   sessions as well. I found the whole experience fascinating, so when Simon was complimentary about
3   my work and urged me to come on board at P & G, my decision was made.
4

5   As it turned out, Simon Clark became my mentor at the firm. He made sure that I got the
6   right assignments and avoided the political pitfalls that exist in every law firm. He also took a special
7   interest in my work and development. Whenever Simon was involved in a big case he requested that
8   I be assigned to work with him. Because I had no family responsibilities I was always available to
9   travel on the firm's business. While I was an associate, Simon became recognized as one of the
10   leading litigators in the firm. Much because of Simon's guidance, I was fast-tracked to a partnership
11   and was made a partner in the firm in 1992, a year before anyone else in my class of associates, and
12   a year before the earliest partnership decisions at P & G are normally made. I believe that Simon was
13   not only responsible for training me and getting me good work to do, but also that he was the driving
14   force in my being made a partner, at least on the fast-track basis.
15

16   While Simon Clark is a role model for me as a lawyer, he does have his Achilles' heel.
17   Although he is married with four children, Simon is well known in the firm for having extramarital
18   affairs with young women in the office. This was especially so in my early years at the firm. It
19   seemed that every few months another rumor would circulate about another affair with either a
20   paralegal or an associate. I don't have much specific information, but I do know of several instances
21   when I was either approached by the young woman involved or where the affair was public.
22

23   One such public affair was with a paralegal by the name of Ellen Dorsen. She and Simon had
24   a relationship that lasted some six months or so, during 1991 and maybe carrying over into 1992.
25   Ms. Dorsen was quite public about the relationship and spoke openly about how she and Simon were
26   doing this or that together. I also overheard her say that Simon was going to leave his wife to marry
27   her. According to the rumor mill, that was Simon's normal *modus operandi*: to promise that he
28   would get a divorce, and then fail to go through with the promise, which usually led to the end of
29   the relationship. I am aware that at some point Simon and Ms. Dorsen broke up, because she was
30   working on a case with me at the time, and I had to ask that she be removed from the case because
31   her work suddenly became very sloppy, which was not the norm for her. I believe that her work
32   never came back to normal and that the firm eventually had to let her go.
33

34   I am also personally aware of two affairs that Simon had with young women associates. I
35   know that he was involved, for a brief time in 1992, with Karen Newman, who was a fourth-year
36   associate with the firm. Karen was well regarded in the firm, but generally not considered
37   partnership material. In the normal course of things, I expect she would have left the firm within a
38   year of when she did, but I suspect, now, that her affair with Simon Clark hastened her leaving. She
39   and Simon worked briefly together on a case that took them to Dallas with some frequency. Because
40   I was not involved in that case I only became aware of their sexual relationship after the fact when
41   Karen approached me to get some advice.
42

43   She told me that she had a brief affair with Simon Clark, but broke it off when it became
44   obvious to her that he had no intention of leaving his wife. She complained to me that her work
45   assignments had dropped off both in terms of quantity (she was having a hard time keeping her
46   billable hours up) and quality (she was assigned to work on several domestic relations matters, which
47   were not considered quality work within the firm) and that she was afraid that she was being

1   sabotaged by Simon Clark. She said she was coming to me because of my relationship with Simon,
2   which was public knowledge. I did not believe that Simon would do such a thing, and I told her so.
3   I did counsel her about her career and when she told me that she felt that she had no realistic
4   opportunity to make partner at P & G, I suggested that a fourth-year associate had very marketable
5   skills and that she should consider moving earlier as opposed to later. I assured her that I could write
6   a letter on her behalf and that I would ask Simon to do so as well. When I asked Simon to write a
7   recommendation for Karen, he told me to draft something for his signature and that he would be glad
8   to help. Shortly thereafter Karen left the firm for a position with another firm in Nita City.
9
10   The only other relationship between Simon and an associate that I have some firsthand
11 knowledge about, other than with Maggie Polisi, was with Carol Merritt. Carol was assigned to one
12 of Simon's cases in 1993 on which I was acting as second chair. The case involved some paper mills
13 in Washington state and a lawsuit by an environmentalist group to halt the harvesting of substantial
14 forests. We spent quite a bit of time in 1993 taking discovery and in motion practice in Washington.
15 Carol was a fourth-year associate and was one of two associates assigned to follow up on discovery
16 and essentially manage the case as it proceeded. Although she was married and the case took her
17 away from home for at least four days of every week, she seemed to enjoy the work and did a quite
18 good job.
19
20   Sometime during the early stages of the case, Simon and Carol began a relationship. They
21 were circumspect in the beginning, but as time went on became quite public about their relationship,
22 at least while they were in Washington. I never saw them together in Nita City. The relationship was
23 serious enough that at some point Carol left her husband. The affair between Carol and Simon lasted
24 about as long as the case, and when the case ended in late 1993, the relationship ended shortly
25 thereafter. Carol took it quite hard, and took about a month's leave from the firm. I know that Simon
26 felt bad about the situation because he called me into his office and explained that Carol had decided
27 not to rejoin the firm. He said he regretted what had happened between them, but that it was just one
28 of those things. He then told me that Carol was back with her husband and that they were moving
29 to Washington, D.C. He asked me to write some glowing recommendations for her, based on her
30 work in the Washington case (which was actually quite good) and send them to a list of his friends
31 in various firms in D.C. I also wrote to some friends of mine and within a few months Carol had
32 joined up with a very good firm in D.C. I believe that she's a partner there now and doing quite well.
33
34   Other than his affair with Maggie Polisi, I have no other specific information about Simon
35 Clark's alleged extramarital activity. In fact, in the years before his relationship with Maggie, I heard
36 very few, if any, rumors about him, but given my relationship with Simon, I don't think that people
37 would consider me a good person with whom to share such gossip. On the other hand, we do work
38 together from time to time and if Simon had a serious affair, especially with someone in the firm,
39 I think I would have heard about it. But P & G is a big firm, so I can't be sure. I know that in 1996
40 Simon's son was in a bad car accident that seriously threatened his life. Simon's concern for his son
41 and the attendant family crisis might also have straightened him out for a while.
42
43   P & G has approximately 330 lawyers, who practice in four sections. The litigation section
44 is the largest with approximately 160 lawyers, less than a third of whom are partners. Within the
45 litigation section, most lawyers work in general commercial litigation. We have a small sub-group
46 that does domestic relations work and another small sub-group that does bankruptcy litigation. The
47 corporate section has approximately 110 lawyers, with the same partner-associate ratio as the

1 litigation section. The tax section has about thirty-five lawyers, about 60 percent of whom are
2 partners. The estate section has approximately twenty lawyers, most of whom are partners.
3
4   As I said earlier, I was the deputy chair of the litigation section of the firm for the almost four
5 years. Simon Clark was the chair for three of those four years. The deputy chair is chosen by the
6 chair, so I started as deputy solely at the discretion of Simon Clark. Our main functions were to
7 oversee client-firm relations and to evaluate the performance of the lawyers in our section of the
8 firm, in particular the associates as they progressed from hiring to partnership. When Simon stepped
9 down as chair in September of 2001, I continued to work as the deputy under the current chair, Rob
10 Bryant, until I left the firm in April of 2002.
11
12   The partnership decision at P & G is based on a series of evaluations of the performance of
13 associates during their time with the firm. I can only speak with specificity about the litigation
14 section of the firm as to how an associate moves from hiring to an offer of partnership. The firm
15 normally hires twenty associates for the litigation section. The normal partnership track is seven to
16 nine years. In the history of the firm, there are two people, myself and Alice Abraham in the tax
17 section of the firm, who have been made partners in six years. By the time that the partnership
18 decision is made, only three or four people from the beginning associates class are considered for
19 partnership. At least 75 percent of the associates who come forward for a partnership decision are
20 successful. The rest of the associates from each class leave the firm to other positions, or are retained
21 by the firm as permanent associates.
22
23   Each associate's performance is evaluated every year, as close in time to the associate's
24 anniversary date as possible. Typically, because most associates begin work in the fall, most
25 evaluations are in September or October. Our system is fairly simple. About a month before the
26 evaluation is to take place, the chair and deputy chair of the litigation section identify from time
27 records the partners for whom the associate has worked during the previous year. Each of those
28 partners are briefly interviewed and asked to evaluate the performance of the associate and to provide
29 any comments on how the associate's performance can improve. The rest of the partnership is also
30 generally solicited to provide any comments they have on any associate. We also consider the
31 number of billable hours the associate has worked. As the partnership decision gets closer the ability
32 of the associate to attract and/or maintain business is also an important factor. The chairman and the
33 deputy then amalgamate all the information and assign a grade of A–F to the associate's performance
34 for the year. That amalgamation is kept in a series of memos written by the chair of the section, or
35 the deputy, to the file of each associate as they progress through the firm. Exhibits 3A–3G are the
36 evaluation memos for Maggie Polisi. Exhibits 5A–5H are the evaluation memos for Mike DeAngelo,
37 although I did not participate in his evaluation for 2002 which took place after I left the firm. The
38 associates are not shown the evaluation memo, but they do receive a letter each year which shows
39 their raise in salary which is tied to the evaluation. Exhibits 4A–4F are Maggie Polisi's salary letters
40 for her time with the firm.
41
42   The A grade is reserved for the most extraordinary of performances, and is generally not
43 awarded until an associate's fifth or sixth year. It is a clear indication that the associate is likely to
44 be offered a partnership sometime in the future. The B grade is, as it usually works out, the best
45 grade associates can receive in their first four years with the firm. It is a sign that the associate is
46 performing very well and is making good progress towards partnership, although partnership is not
47 mentioned in evaluations until the fifth year. Only about three to five members of each associates

1   class receive B grades in their first through fourth years. The B grade in the fifth year and beyond
2   is still considered excellent, but generally connotes that the associate is borderline for partnership.
3   An associate will typically receive at least one grade of A before they are considered for partnership,
4   and most typically in the year in which they come up for partnership.
5

6   The C grade is the typical grade received in the first two years of an associate's career. It
7   reflects a good, but not exemplary, performance. The C grade in years three and four, is usually a
8   good indicator that the associate will not be made a partner and associates with a C grade in his or
9   her fourth year are typically advised that it would be appropriate for them to seek other employment.
10 In some cases, an associate will be particularly bright and do very well in analysis of legal issues,
11 but fail to have the necessary communication and advocacy skills to become a litigation partner in
12 the firm. In those cases, the associate may be approached with an offer as a permanent associate.
13 Permanent associates have no possibility of being made partners and are salaried employees of the
14 firm paid at approximately the same level as a sixth-year associate on the partnership track. A grade
15 of C in the fifth year is usually a clear sign that the associate will not make partner. With some of
16 these associates, the firm will make efforts to place them in general counsel offices of our good
17 clients. Those positions pay very well and usually have excellent benefits. It is the firm's interest to
18 place former associates with clients in that it fosters good client relations. In fact, I have several
19 former P & G associates working for me at NCW in the General Counsel's office.
20

21   The D grade is given for below expectation performance. While it is possible for an associate
22 to have a D grade in the first year and improve and eventually go on to partnership, a D in the first
23 two years will usually result in a recommendation to seek other employment. A grade of D in each
24 of the first three years results in the setting of a termination date, usually thirty days after the
25 evaluation.
26

27   The F grade is reserved for situations where the associate has performed in an incompetent
28 manner. Because we are very careful in our hiring decisions, I know of no associate who has ever
29 received an F grade in an evaluation.
30

31   Once the grade has been assigned, the chair of the section, the deputy chair of the section,
32 and the associate meet for the purpose of the evaluation. The associate is first given his or her grade
33 for the year and then is given an explanation of the basis for the grade. The source of individual
34 partner comments is not divulged to the associate, but the nature of the comment often serves to
35 identify its source. During the meeting the section chair will read the amalgamation of the comments
36 that have been prepared by the chair and the deputy chair. If questions are asked, the chair may refer
37 to notes from interviews with individual partners, but that is not the norm. The associate is then
38 given an opportunity to comment on the evaluation or ask questions. The associate is then told their
39 raise for the next year. The associate does not receive any written evaluation. The only record that
40 is kept is the amalgamation of the comments from the partners and the records on billable hours.
41 Individual interview notes are destroyed after the evaluation meeting. In addition, once an associate
42 is made a partner, the only records that are maintained are those of the grades assigned for each year
43 and their billable hours for each year. Once an associate leaves the firm, the records of grades and
44 billable hours are kept for approximately five or six years, in case the firm is contacted for a letter
45 of recommendation for another position. The evaluation memos are destroyed once the associate
46 leaves the firm. Exhibits 7A and 7B are a compilation of the records concerning the class of

1   associates at P & G who began as associates in 1994. It shows the billable hours and grades for each
2   associate in that class during their time at P & G.
3
4   While the associate does not get a copy of the evaluation record, they do receive, as I said
5   earlier, a written confirmation of their raise. Raises are based on a set formula, that coincides with
6   the grade that the associate has received. The raise scale is as follows: A - 7%; B - 5%; C - 3%; and
7   D - 2%. Salaries are also adjusted periodically to reflect increases in base salary. These increases are
8   irrespective of merit and are reflected on the salary letters as market adjustments.
9
10   Partnership decisions are usually made in June of the seventh year of an associate's tenure
11   with the firm. In order for an associate to be made a partner, the associate must be nominated by the
12   partners in their section. The nomination is by majority vote. That nomination goes to the Executive
13   Committee of the firm. The Executive Committee then recommends the associate to the entire
14   partnership. The Executive Committee normally implements the recommendations of the four
15   sections of the firm (litigation, corporate, tax and estates) unless in the committee's opinion the
16   particular section is too top-heavy with partners. During my time at the firm, I know of no occasion
17   when the Executive Committee has not recommended for partnership an associate who has been
18   nominated by his or her section, although I believe there was one circumstance where an associate
19   was made to wait a year by the Executive Committee before they were recommended to the entire
20   partnership. The recommendation of the executive committee is then voted on by all partners. A
21   majority vote is required to achieve partnership. It is very unusual for the entire partnership to vote
22   down an associate who has been recommended by both his or her section and the Executive
23   Committee. In my time at P & G that has only happened twice.
24
25   I first met Maggie Polisi when she came to work as a paralegal at the firm at about the same
26   time that I started as an associate. I didn't have very much to do with her until 1988 when she was
27   assigned to work one of Simon Clark's cases to which I was also assigned. This case, involving a
28   dispute among the largest banks in the state of Nita, was extremely complex and involved difficult
29   legal issues. It was the case in which Simon Clark established himself as one of the best, if not the
30   best, litigators and trial lawyers in the firm, and probably in the city as well. Maggie was chosen to
31   work as one of the trial paralegals when the case came to trial in January of 1990. As a fourth-year
32   associate, I was assigned to coordinate between the two partners who were trying the case and the
33   paralegals. During that trial, Maggie and I got to work quite closely together, and I was very
34   impressed with her intellect and how quickly she was able to assimilate and understand directions
35   given to her, and anticipate other needs in the trial. Simon Clark was also impressed with Maggie's
36   work and I know that he encouraged her to apply to law school, which she did. Since she was
37   applying to Nita University School of Law, as an alumni I volunteered to write a recommendation
38   letter for her.
39
40   Maggie was accepted to Nita law school and attended the evening division. This was
41   necessary because she was a single mother of small children and she needed to support them while
42   she attended school. She continued to work as a paralegal at P & G during her first year of law
43   school. As it turned out, she did very well in school and we offered her a position as a law clerk with
44   the firm, which meant a pay raise for her. During her four years of law school, Maggie did quite a
45   lot of work for me. She was bright, insightful, and talented. I remember that I called Simon's
46   attention to her work from time to time and kept him posted on all of Maggie's success in law
47   school. He was thoughtful enough to compliment her work as I did, but I know coming from Simon

1   Clark, it meant more to her. As it turned out she graduated magna cum laude, finished first in her
2   class and was an editor of the law review; all while working full time at P & G and having the
3   responsibilities of a single mother.
4
5   As you can tell I was, and am, quite a fan of Maggie Polisi. In the early fall of her fourth and
6   final year of law school, unbeknownst to her, I went to Simon Clark and spoke on Maggie's behalf
7   about her getting a position as an associate with P & G. Although Simon didn't embrace the idea
8   immediately, he thought it worth checking out with the hiring committee. P & G had never hired one
9   of its law clerks as an associate, as a matter of policy, and had never hired a graduate of Nita Law
10   School's evening division, I guess based on some misconception that the evening division is
11   somehow different than the day division in quality of education. Not hiring law clerks made sense
12   as a matter of policy in that it kept competition among the law clerks, which might have interfered
13   with productivity, at a minimum. Not hiring graduates of the evening division of Nita Law School
14   made no sense at all. At least at Nita University, the law curriculum is taught by the same instructors
15   in the day and evening division and no distinction is made between the divisions. If anything,
16   because the evening division students all have demanding day jobs, their accomplishments at law
17   school are more commendable, not less.
18
19   Simon and I quietly circulated the idea around the hiring committee, of which I was a
20   member and Simon was the chair, and most people on the committee seemed amenable to recruiting
21   Maggie. Our job was made easier by the fact that the summer associates from the previous summer
22   were less impressive than usual and that it looked that our yield of full-time associates from that
23   group would be lower than usual.
24
25   We approached Maggie with the idea of applying to P & G and she seemed genuinely
26   flattered. She did end up applying and going through the formal interviewing process. Maggie easily
27   made it through the preliminary interviews and was invited to the firm for a full day of interviews.
28   She apparently did quite well. Given that we already knew the high quality of her work, as supported
29   by Simon Clark, who was known in the firm as being very demanding, in many ways Maggie was
30   a much more certain product than someone who had only spent a summer with us, or someone who
31   had never worked in the firm.
32
33   The only major stumbling block was Maggie's insistence, given her responsibilities as a
34   single parent, that she not be assigned to any cases that took her our of Nita City for extended
35   periods of time. Because P & G had and has a national practice, this requirement somewhat limited
36   the range of matters on which Maggie could work, and this caused problems with several of my
37   partners, the most vocal of whom was Jayne Post. This seemed odd in that Jayne worked exclusively
38   on domestic relations matters, that were almost always local in nature, but her complaint did have
39   some merit. Simon and I argued on Maggie's behalf, that there was plenty of work of varying
40   complexity in and around Nita City, and that after all, the children would eventually grow up and
41   leave the house. That argument seemed to carry the day. There were also some questions asked about
42   the quality of the education in the evening division of Nita law school, but I was able to answer those
43   questions sufficiently to remove that as an impediment.
44
45   The committee eventually voted to offer Maggie a position as an associate. Simon Clark
46   made the offer personally and Maggie accepted. She later thanked me for all my help, and told me
47   that she would prove that our confidence in her was deserved. Maggie did come to see me in July

1   of 1994 when she received the formal letter from the firm which set her salary. She was concerned
2   that the language of the letter could be interpreted so that she could be required to travel extensively,
3   despite the clear understanding that she had with the firm. (SEE EXHIBIT 2) I assured her that the
4   firm was well aware of her special requirements and not to worry about the letter, that it was just a
5   form letter.
6
7   I became a mentor of sorts for Maggie Polisi. I knew how important Simon's guidance had
8   been for me as I worked myself up through the firm to partnership, and I thought that I could give
9   Maggie similar guidance. I felt a special responsibility towards her because I had recruited her to the
10   firm, and because she was a graduate of my law school. I knew that there could be added pressure
11   on an associate who was the first from a particular school to work at the firm, or in her case, the first
12   from the evening division of Nita U., because of how it felt for me when I was the first associate
13   from the law school at P & G. In addition, I liked Maggie as a person, and admired the way that she
14   had worked her way through law school, while at the same time having the responsibilities of being
15   a single mother.
16
17   I also talked up Maggie among my partners so that they would request her to work on various
18   projects. I was confident of Maggie's abilities, and with the right opportunities, I was sure that she
19   would flourish at the firm. I also warned her to avoid being pigeonholed in less-desirable specialties
20   within the firm. For example, within the litigation section of the firm, the vast majority of lawyers
21   work in general commercial litigation which involves the full range of problems faced by our large
22   corporate clients. There were, at the time that Maggie joined the firm, and there remain today, two
23   small sub-groups within the litigation section: a domestic relations group headed by Jayne Post and
24   a bankruptcy group headed by John Crandall. These sub-groups, because of their size and specialty,
25   carried less clout than general litigation and it was, while I was with the firm, much harder to
26   become a partner if an associate specialized in either of those groups than if they worked on general
27   commercial litigation matters. First, the associate's work is exposed to a broader range of lawyers,
28   and second, the work is thought of as having greater complexity and requiring higher analytical
29   skills. These perceptions may have been inaccurate, but because they existed, they might as well
30   have been real.
31
32   The domestic relations sub-group was a particularly bad choice for women associates because
33   many of the older members of the firm viewed that practice with disdain, referring to it in a
34   derogatory way as "women's work." Now that you ask, it's true that while I was with the firm, the
35   only women partners in the litigation section were in those two areas.
36
37   I did my best to guide Maggie through the political minefields of the law firm, and she
38   seemed grateful for my help. She also followed my advice most of the time, and through the first
39   four years of her practice at P & G she did quite well. She was given good assignments, and
40   impressed most of the partners for whom she worked. She worked for me on a number of cases in
41   that period and did terrific work. There was some mild criticism of her writing in her first year, but
42   that was typical of almost all of our associates. I believe she was graded at the C level in her first
43   year, which put her in the top half of her associates class. I recall that she was upset with her
44   evaluation, but I told her not to be, that the grade was typical and that she should just keep on doing
45   good work and she would be fine.
46

1   In Maggie's second, third and fourth years she was graded at the B level, which I believe put
2   her in the top three or four of her associates class. Her evaluations were uniformly good, and
3   although I did help her get good assignments when I could, she was in demand by other partners as
4   well. There were very few negative comments. A couple of the old-timers at the firm, would, from
5   time to time, complain about her not being "aggressive" or "tough" enough, which I believe was a
6   code for "she's a woman," but those comments should not have been taken seriously and I told
7   Maggie as much. The one negative comment that had some substance came from Jayne Post, who
8   felt that it was inappropriate for Maggie to confine her practice to cases that kept her in Nita City,
9   or at least required minimum time out of town. Jayne felt that Maggie's lack of travel created a
10   burden on other associates, and kept the firm from being able to evaluate how Maggie performed
11   with the added stress of having to work in unfamiliar places, dealing with an unfamiliar bench and
12   bar. She felt this evaluation was important because so much of P & G's practice was outside of Nita
13   City, and if Maggie made partner she would be expected to travel where her cases took her. When
14   I reminded Jayne that the travel issue had been raised, discussed, and decided when Maggie was
15   interviewing with the firm, her response was that the children had to be old enough at that time to
16   be able to deal with child-care help in the home when Maggie was required to travel.
17
18   Maggie had a terrible fifth year as an associate, and it could not have come at a worse time.
19   By the time an associate is in her fifth year the partners take a very close look at her performance.
20   This is because by this point the associate is fully trained and is dealing with relatively complex
21   factual settings involving difficult analytical issues. As a result, the fifth year usually provides an
22   excellent marker for partnership potential, Maggie's terrible year, however, was really not a
23   reflection of abilities, but caused by a series of personal problems.
24
25   As I understand it, both of Maggie's children, who were teenagers at the time, went through
26   difficult periods, while at the same time her father was diagnosed with cancer and died. The
27   coincidence of these events kept Maggie from being focused on her work. Her billable hours dipped
28   significantly, and quite frankly the quality of her work diminished as well. Because I was aware of
29   her personal situation, I covered for her on the work she was doing for me, but other partners were
30   less generous in evaluating her work product. This was even though they were aware of Maggie's
31   personal problems. Their complaint was that at P & G the pressure of the practice and the need to
32   perform at a high level does not diminish because a lawyer has personal problems. They expressed
33   concern that a pattern of such behavior at the onset of personal crises would develop, and that was
34   a problem. I was privy to all of these comments because by that time, in 1999, Simon Clark was
35   made the chair of the litigation section, and he asked me to be his deputy.
36
37   The end result of Maggie's evaluation was that she was graded at the C level for the year.
38   The partners in the litigation section authorized Simon to use his influence to place her in the general
39   counsel's office of one of our client companies, or agree to give her a strong recommendation should
40   she choose to seek alternative employment herself. Some of the partners in the section felt that those
41   should be Maggie's only two options. Mainly because of my faith in Maggie and her ability, and at
42   my insistence, Simon persuaded the litigation partners that Maggie should be given a shot at
43   redeeming herself by working on a very important antitrust case of his that was heating up for one
44   of our best clients, Nita Computer World (NCW). If it had not been for Simon Clark, Maggie's
45   career with P & G would have ended in 1999. That's why what happened to Maggie later on was so
46   ironic.
47

1   Simon and I presented Maggie with her evaluation and with the options available to her.
2   Although she was disappointed with her grade, she opted to work on the NCW litigation, as I knew
3   she would. No one can doubt the heart of Maggie Polisi.
4
5   I was not involved in the NCW antitrust case, but I got periodic reports from Simon on
6   Maggie's performance. As I predicted, she performed magnificently, according to Simon, and he
7   complimented me on my judgment. Around the end of 1999 or the beginning of 2000, I had a
8   conversation with Simon Clark about Maggie Polisi. He confirmed that she was still doing a great
9   job, but that he was interested in finding out what I knew about Maggie's personal life. I told him
10 about her children, but I knew that he was aware of them and the problems Maggie had with them
11 the previous year. He asked whether I knew if she was involved with anyone romantically, and I
12 answered honestly that I didn't know. It was obvious that Simon's interest in Maggie went beyond
13 the professional.
14
15   For some reason I felt very protective towards Maggie, and told Simon that if he was
16 interested in her, other than as a lawyer, that he had better be serious, because I felt that she was very
17 vulnerable at the time. I asked him not to take advantage of her. Simon smiled and asked me whether
18 there was anything going on between Maggie and me, and I, of course, told him there wasn't. He
19 then said that I shouldn't worry about Maggie, that she was a big girl and could handle herself, but
20 told me that I shouldn't worry, that he would "be gentle." I must have visibly bristled, because he
21 then said, "Don't worry, everything will work out fine." Simon then moved on to other matters
22 involving the litigation section administration, signaling that the conversation about Maggie was
23 over.
24
25   During the early spring of 2000, it became obvious to me that a relationship other than
26 professional was developing between Maggie and Simon. They were always out of town together
27 on the NCW case, and they were inseparable when they were in the office. The rumors of another
28 Simon Clark affair started to buzz around the office, and although I wasn't certain that anything was
29 going on, the signs were all there.
30
31   At the same time the NCW case was apparently progressing very well, and according to
32 Simon, Maggie had performed brilliantly. When the case settled on extremely favorable terms to
33 NCW in June of 2000, the client was so happy that the entire litigation team and spouses were
34 invited to a week's vacation in the Bahamas at the client's expense. It was at this vacation that the
35 affair between Simon and Maggie became public knowledge within the firm. According to others
36 from the firm, Maggie and Simon were in each other's company constantly, from the earliest in the
37 morning until the latest at night. They were also seen strolling arm in arm on the beach. When they
38 returned, their relationship was obvious to everyone.
39
40   Given Simon's history, I felt that it was my responsibility as Maggie's friend and one of her
41 mentors to counsel her about the risk attendant her relationship with Simon Clark. I asked Maggie
42 whether she was aware of Simon's history with other women at the firm and she told me that she
43 was. She told me that this time it was different, that Simon was going to leave his wife once his
44 youngest son went away to college. I responded by saying something like "he's said that before,"
45 and Maggie told me she didn't want to discuss the matter any further. I did tell her that I hoped
46 everything worked out for her, but that if it didn't that I didn't think that I could protect her interests
47 at the firm. She looked sort of stunned, but just said thanks for my concern and I left. My statement

1 to her was meant to convey the fact that there was some risk that her future at the firm would be
2 compromised if it was viewed that her continued employment was contrary to Simon Clark's wishes.
3 I can't say that Simon ever personally got an associate or paralegal with whom he was romantically
4 involved dismissed from the firm, but I do believe that my partners would do whatever they thought
5 was necessary to keep Simon Clark happy. After all, he was a major source of business for the firm,
6 and we couldn't afford to lose him. I also know of no woman at the firm, either lawyer or paralegal,
7 who survived professionally after an affair with Simon Clark.
8
9 Because of the work Maggie had done on NCW, as reported effusively by Simon Clark, and
10 maybe because some of the lower level partners wanted to get on Simon's good side, Maggie was
11 very much in demand for very high-quality assignments during the summer of 2000. She apparently
12 performed very well because all reports on her during her sixth-year evaluation process were
13 glowing. In addition, the general counsel at NCW wrote a letter congratulating the entire litigation
14 team, but giving special praise to Maggie. (SEE EXHIBIT 6) Several of the other partners in the
15 litigation section even congratulated me on my good judgment in backing Maggie so strongly the
16 previous year. Because of the high praise for her work and enormous number of billable hours,
17 Maggie was graded at the A level for her sixth year, which as I said is a strong positive indicator for
18 a favorable partnership decision in the seventh year. We, of course, informed Maggie of that fact and
19 she seemed very pleased. Simon came around the desk and gave her a big hug and a kiss. Maggie
20 looked a little embarrassed that Simon did that when I was in the room, so I just congratulated her
21 and went back to my office.
22
23 During the fall of 2000, Maggie was assigned to work on another case for NCW on which
24 I was the lead partner. It was no where near as complex as the one the previous year, but it did give
25 her another chance to show her talent. It also involved a similar issue of protecting NCW's trade
26 secrets that was involved in the previous case that Maggie handled. She took good advantage of the
27 opportunity and performed very well, at least during the fall of 2000.
28
29 In the early part of 2001, the inevitable happened and Simon Clark ended his affair with
30 Maggie Polisi. Maggie went into an apparently rather deep depression. For the next several months
31 her work was off and she seemed to be constantly suffering from a cold or the flu. As a result, the
32 requests for her to work on cases also dropped off. It's possible that the drop off in work requests
33 was also a result of the rather public break-up of Simon and Maggie. Just as some partners might try
34 to curry favor with Simon by asking for Maggie when they knew she was involved with him, the
35 opposite might also be true. I do not believe that Simon Clark was directly responsible for the drop-
36 off in Maggie's assignments in that I never heard anyone say that Simon had approached them, but
37 as I said, my partners might have reacted to what they thought was what Simon wanted. I just don't
38 know.
39
40 At any rate, when I started to collect information for a partnership vote by the litigation
41 section on the four people eligible for partnership that year, I started to receive some negative
42 evaluations of Maggie's work. I also noted that her billable hours were sharply lower. She had billed
43 850 hours for September 2000 through January 2001 and only 550 hours for the four months
44 leading up to her evaluation. In addition I started hearing questions again about her toughness and
45 resiliency, and her ability to not let personal matters interfere with her work. There were even some
46 questions raised about her intellectual ability, which I hadn't heard since Maggie's first year with

1   the firm. And even though the NCW case should have answered any questions about how she
2   performed when in unfamiliar settings, those criticisms also resurfaced, especially from Jayne Post.
3
4   I can't prove that Simon Clark did or said anything overtly about Maggie that caused the
5   negative evaluations. He really wouldn't need to. After he and Maggie broke up, it was public
6   information and some of my colleagues might have evaluated Maggie negatively to try to please
7   Simon Clark. The break-up could certainly explain her drop-off in assignments as many of my
8   partners wouldn't want to appear to weigh in favor of Maggie if there was a problem with Simon.
9
10   I approached Maggie with the bad news I was receiving. While I was not specific, I gave her
11   the gist of the negative comments I was receiving about her. I also noted the sharp drop-off in
12   billable hours. Maggie said that she just hadn't gotten a lot of assignments. I asked her why she
13   hadn't come to me, and she said she really didn't think anything of it at the time, that she thought
14   it was just a down work cycle. I wish she had said something or I had been more attentive. Lack of
15   billables became a strong issue for Maggie's opponents. I gave her my best advice and told her that
16   in my opinion it was not a good idea to push for partnership that year. I did tell her that if she chose
17   to go forward that I would support her nomination for partnership by the litigation section, but that
18   she would be in a much better position if she waited a year and repeated her sixth year performance.
19   I assured her I would make certain she got the right assignments to showcase her talents. She didn't
20   speak right away, and when she did, she asked whether Simon Clark had anything to do with her
21   negative evaluation. When I didn't answer immediately she just said "never mind, I'll get back to
22   you in a couple of days," and I left her office.
23
24   Several days later Maggie came by my office and told me that she wanted to go forward with
25   a decision that year. I again tried to talk her out of it, but her mind was made up so I told her I'd do
26   what she wished, and that she had my support. Simon had asked me to prepare the evaluation of
27   Maggie and I did. Her evaluation was really in two parts. Her work was excellent during the fall, and
28   then fell off in the winter and spring. As a result, I graded her at the B level.
29
30   The four people up for partnership nomination that year from the litigation section were
31   Roger Kramer, Mark Hancock, Michael DeAngelo, and Maggie. The meeting began on a Thursday
32   afternoon with a consideration of Michael DeAngelo. Mike had consistently been graded at the B
33   level in his evaluations. Although not regarded as a superstar, he was considered as a rock-solid
34   performer with uniformly good skills. There was some question about his ability to attract business
35   and also about how he did on client relations. The question about client relations seemed to hang up
36   the partnership and we went round and round on the matter. There was also the usual argument about
37   whether being solid is enough, especially in a year when there were other candidates for partnership
38   who had all scored in the A range, at least for one year. In the end, the partnership sent me back to
39   Mike with a suggestion that he hold off for another year. The next year's class was not nearly so
40   strong, and it would also give Mike another year to improve his evaluation. Although reluctant, Mike
41   accepted the recommendation and withdrew for consideration in 2001. As it turned out it was a very
42   good move on his part as the reports on Mike's performance for the second half of 2001 were terrific
43   and continued through 2002. In addition he was able to attract a good sized client to the firm. I
44   understand that he eventually was made a partnership offer in June of 2002.
45
46   Mark Hancock was an easy case. He too consistently received solid B evaluations, and
47   although not brilliant was a solid performer. What distinguished Mark was his courtroom ability.

1   During the spring of 2001, he conducted devastating cross-examinations of several witnesses that
2   his mentor credited for winning the case in a very important interference with contract matter for one
3   of our best clients. The client was present during the examinations, and specifically requested that
4   Mark be on any trial team for a case for that client. His trial performance rated him an A for his
5   seventh year, and the client's insistence on his being on future trial teams made him a lock for
6   partnership. He was nominated after a brief discussion, that mostly praised his abilities.
7
8   Roger Kramer was next, and he too was an easy case. Roger was generally considered one
9   of the smartest lawyers in the firm. He had received A evaluations in both his fifth and sixth years.
10 Roger was also very personable and did very well with the clients on whose cases he worked. He
11 was also the son of the president of one of our better clients, who we felt we would certainly lose
12 if Roger was not with the firm. His billable hours were good, but if he had a weakness it was in that
13 area. The only real question with Roger was whether he should have received a partnership offer in
14 his sixth year. As expected, Roger breezed through.
15
16   The meeting then adjourned until Friday afternoon for the consideration of Maggie's
17 candidacy. The meeting began at approximately 3:00 p.m. and lasted until 8:00 p.m. Maggie had a
18 number of very strong supporters, including myself, who thought she possessed a great combination
19 of skills and that she would do great work on anything to which she was assigned. Her detractors
20 raised all of the issues I mentioned before, Jayne Post being one of the most vociferous, and the
21 debate was long and rancorous. Simon Clark, who chaired the meeting as chair of the section spoke
22 very little. He did speak about Maggie's work on the NCW case in glowing terms, but admitted that
23 Maggie's performance in 2001 was troublesome. As chair of the section, he was not required to vote,
24 but announced that he was going to abstain in the vote. His abstention, in my opinion, was the
25 equivalent of a negative vote and probably was one of the determining factors in the outcome. In the
26 end, however, the feeling that Maggie had been inconsistent in her performance, that in the view of
27 some, reflected a lack of toughness and resiliency, plus the fact that she was not in a position to
28 attract any business to the firm, carried the day. In a close vote her nomination for partnership was
29 denied. I tried to get the partnership to allow her another year to improve her performance, but the
30 litigation partners seemed to not have the stomach for a repeat of that meeting in a year. I was told
31 to inform Maggie that she had six months to find another position.
32
33   I found Maggie in her office when the meeting ended. She took the news fairly hard. She
34 asked if she could have another year to improve, but I told her that the decision was final. She did
35 ask about what Simon's position at the meeting was, and I told her that I couldn't divulge individual
36 comments as a matter of policy. I told her I was sorry, that I had done my best, but that there was
37 nothing I could do.
38
39   After the meeting, I ran into Simon Clark outside his office. He asked me to come in for a
40 drink which I did. He asked if I had gotten up with Maggie and I told him I had, and that she had
41 taken the news pretty hard. He knew that Maggie was a favorite of mine and he asked how I was
42 doing. Something snapped, and I lit into him. I told him that he was an egomaniac and that if he had
43 exercised a little control of his libido that Maggie would be a partner today. I told him that he was
44 a real jerk and that he had ruined a terrific legal career. Simon looked shocked. I had never talked
45 to him that way before. He didn't deny my accusation, but he did say that it was Maggie who had
46 ended the relationship, not him, and that he was sorry about how it had worked out. He said that he
47 knew how I felt about Maggie and again said he was sorry, but this time to me. I told Simon that I

1 would draft a recommendation letter for him concerning Maggie, in order to help her in securing a
2 new position. He said that was fine. I then got up and walked out of Simon's office.
3
4   Ever since that day my relationship with Simon Clark has been different. Although we still
5 interacted on business matters in a fairly regular way, the closeness we once had was gone, and, to
6 be honest, I lost some respect for him. I think the same is true at the firm, because in September of
7 2001, Simon was replaced as the chief of the litigation section after only three years in the position.
8 The normal term for that position is five years. When the announcement was made by the Executive
9 Committee of the firm of the change in leadership, it was couched in an explanation that Simon's
10 trial schedule was too demanding to allow him sufficient time to administer the section, but the
11 gossip in the firm is that the whole situation with Maggie was the straw that broke the camel's back
12 as far as tolerance for Simon's dalliances. The new chief of the division is Rob Bryant. He asked me
13 to stay on as deputy for purposes of continuity and I agreed to do so.
14
15   Maggie did not handle the situation of her firing well. Although she interviewed for jobs with
16 other firms, nothing came of it. Originally I thought that her confidence had been undermined by the
17 whole episode at P & G, and that probably affected her interviewing skills. I now know that in a
18 couple of circumstances that Simon Clark had done her in with a poor reference letter. I only found
19 out about the letters in January of 2002 when Maggie called me to tell me that she had a copy of a
20 letter written by Simon to John Randall of the Morrison firm in Nita City which was far from
21 complimentary. She read the letter to me, including some hand written comments that I now
22 recognize to be in Simon's handwriting. (SEE EXHIBIT 11) I felt really bad about this because I had
23 given Maggie a copy of the letter that I had drafted for Simon's signature, and had encouraged her
24 to use him as a reference. (SEE EXHIBIT 10) I know that he had never been vindictive in any
25 previous ending of an affair, so I was really surprised that he was regarding Maggie. When I
26 confronted him with the fact that he didn't use my letter, Simon became very defensive and told me
27 to mind my own business. Since that time I have lost what respect I had for Simon personally,
28 although I have to concede to him his legal abilities.
29
30   I also know that Maggie tried to get a teaching job. Although she had some interviews at the
31 law school hiring convention, the only thing that came of it initially was an adjunct teaching position
32 at the University of Nita School of Law. Because I knew that adjuncts did not make much money,
33 I offered to help Maggie out financially with whatever kind of loan she needed. She turned down my
34 offer. Eventually Maggie ended up with teaching offers from both Nita University and Conwell
35 University, although it took a while for them to come in. I'm happy to say that she returned to her
36 and my alma mater, where I'm sure she will be a great success.
37
38   I also know that she filed a complaint against the firm with the EEOC. Although we did not talk
39 directly about that fact at the time, the firm did receive notice of her allegations in the summer of 2001.
40 (SEE EXHIBIT 14) As the deputy of the litigation section, I was contacted to be sure to maintain
41 whatever files we still had on Maggie and the other people who came up for partner in 2001. We had
42 the paragraph evaluations on Maggie and Mike DeAngelo because they were still associates at the
43 time the firm received the EEOC letter. Because Mark Hancock and Roger Kramer had been made
44 partners by that time, the only records we had on them for their years as associates were on their
45 grades and their billable hours. The same was true of former associates from Maggie's class who had
46 left the firm. (SEE EXHIBITS 7A and 7B) The firm returned the EEOC notice with a general denial

1 written by Rob Bryant. (SEE EXHIBIT 15) Sometime in early January of 2002 we received a copy
2 of the EEOC's "right to sue" letter that was sent to Maggie. (SEE EXHIBIT 16)
3
4   Maggie resigned in December of 2001 when her six-month grace period with the firm ended.
5 I asked if there was anything I could do and she told me no, that she thought everything would work
6 out. As I said, I know I told her that if she needed a loan I was always available. She thanked me but
7 said that she didn't think that would be necessary. I told her that I was aware of her complaint to the
8 EEOC and said that I would be willing to testify on her behalf if the need ever arose. She gave me
9 a hug and left the firm.
10
11   The whole matter with Maggie Polisi has left a sour taste in my mouth for the politics of P
12 & G, so when I was approached by NCW about my current job, I pursued the opportunity. I was
13 surprised that it was so easy for me to leave P & G, but I guess the time was right. I have a terrific
14 job at NCW where I oversee the entire legal department of about twenty-five lawyers, and also
15 oversee our litigation which is farmed out to P & G. Simon Clark still handles our most important
16 matters and I interact with him professionally, but we have no personal relationship any longer. I
17 have not talked to him about Maggie's lawsuit against the firm, nor have I talked with P & G's
18 lawyers.
19
20   When I got the job at NCW, one of the first people I tried to hire into our legal department
21 was Maggie Polisi. At the time I offered her the job, in May of 2002, she had already accepted the
22 teaching position at Nita University, so she turned me down. I told her that there would always be
23 a position for her at NCW if she ever changed her mind. Maggie and I continue to see each other
24 socially from time to time. We are good friends. I'll have to admit, because you've asked, that I
25 would be interested in a romantic relationship with her, but we have never interacted in that way,
26 and I don't expect that we ever will.
27

I have read this deposition and it is complete and accurate.

Clifford Fuller
Clifford Fuller

Subscribed and sworn before me this 9th day of December, 2002.

Harry Gibbons
Harry Gibbons CSR
Certified Shorthand Reporter

This deposition was given under oath at the offices of the defendant's counsel on November 20, 2002. This deposition was given under oath, read and signed by the deponent.

DEPOSITION OF SIMON CLARK

1   My name is Simon Clark. I am fifty-two years old and married. My wife Amanda and I have
2   four children: Marla, who is twenty-eight; Simon Jr., who is twenty-four; Nora, who is twenty-three;
3   and Spencer, who is nineteen. Marla has a son, Grant, who is my only grandchild. I am a partner in
4   the law firm of Parker & Gould (P & G) here in Nita City. I have recently stepped down as the chair
5   of the litigation section, after a three year term. I practice in the litigation section, and I am
6   considered one of the top trial lawyers and litigators at the firm. I am a member of the American
7   College of Trial Lawyers and the International Society of Barristers. I am also on the Board of
8   Directors of the Nita Chapter of the ACLU. My practice is a national practice and I have tried cases
9   in approximately twelve different states.
10
11   I am a 1973 graduate of Harvard University and a 1976 graduate of the Harvard Law School.
12   After graduating from law school I worked for three years in the civil division of the U.S.
13   Department of Justice in Washington, D.C. In 1979, I joined P & G as an associate and four years
14   later was made a partner in the litigation section of the firm, where I have worked ever since.
15
16   P & G is a 330-lawyer law firm. Our only office is in Nita City. We are one of the largest
17   firms in the city and like to think of ourselves as one of the best. There are four sections in the firm:
18   litigation, corporate, tax and estates. The litigation section is the largest with approximately 160
19   lawyers, a third of whom are partners. Corporate is the next largest with about 110 lawyers. The tax
20   section has about thirty-five lawyers and the estate section about twenty. Most of the litigation
21   section works in general commercial litigation matters. There are two small sub-groups in the
22   litigation section: domestic relations and bankruptcy. Jayne Post heads up the domestic relations
23   group and John Crandall heads up the bankruptcy group, although that will likely change this year
24   when two well-qualified women associates come up for partnership. It is true that there are no
25   women partners in the litigation section who work in general litigation. Jayne Post has three other
26   women partners in domestic relations (Sherry Barker, Ann Feinman, and Georgia Bratton), and John
27   Crandall has two women partners (Cheryl Stein and Kathryn Kowalski) in bankruptcy. In the past
28   those sub-groups within litigation were not considered as having the same quality of practice as in
29   general litigation, but in my opinion, Jayne and John have done terrific jobs in building their
30   practices, and although their practices are different than a general litigation practice, they are well
31   respected within the firm. To date, all partners at P & G are equity partners. We have discussed using
32   the designation of non-equity partner for someone with excellent all-around skills as a lawyer but
33   without the ability to attract or maintain clients. To date that circumstance has not arisen.
34
35   Since I was the Chief of the Litigation Section of the firm, who has responsibility for
36   administering the evaluation and partnership decisions in the firm, I can describe the process that we
37   utilize to evaluate associates. Each associate is evaluated yearly on his anniversary date. In the
38   litigation section the chief and deputy chief of the section identify the partners for whom the
39   associate has worked in the previous year and interview those partners to get their evaluations of the
40   associate's performance. We also solicit the partners generally for additional comments. Those
41   comments and the billable hours for the associate are then compiled into a summary and the
42   associate is assigned a grade of A to F. Exhibits 3A–3G are the evaluation summaries for Maggie
43   Polisi, and Exhibits 5A–5G are the evaluation summaries for Michael DeAngelo, who was in
44   Maggie's class. I prepared several of those memos when I was the chair of the litigation section. The

1   compilation of comments and grades are given to all partners in the section for comments. The chief
2   and the deputy then meet with the associate and communicate the grade and the underlying basis for
3   the grade. We do not divulge the source of comments although sometime the comment or the context
4   of the comment will indicate who made it. We also tell the associate how many people in his class
5   of associates (which usually begins with approximately twenty people) received either the same
6   grade or a higher grade. The associate does not receive a copy of the evaluation memos, and they
7   are destroyed when the associate either leaves the firm, or is made partner. The only records we
8   maintain are as to the grade and billable hours each associate receives. Exhibits 7A and 7B are a
9   compilation of the hours and grades for those associates who were in Maggie Polisi's associates
10 class.
11
12   The normal partnership track at P & G is seven or eight years. Most people who make partner
13 will have received a grade of B for at least two of their first four years, and B's or A's in their last
14 three or four years before the partnership decision is made. It is unusual for a associate who makes
15 partner not to have at least one A grade, usually within a year of the partnership decision. In addition
16 to the grades earned, the potential ability of the associate to attract business to the firm is also an
17 important factor at the time the partnership decision is made.
18
19   The litigation section nominates its associates for partnership to the Executive Committee
20 of the firm, which then presents the candidates to the entire partnership for its consideration. For an
21 associate to be made a partner, he must receive a majority vote of the entire partnership, but the
22 nominations of the sections are usually followed except in extraordinary circumstances.
23
24   Those associates who do not meet the above criteria leave the firm in a variety of ways. Some
25 associates are identified as not having partnership potential because of our evaluation that they
26 would not interact well with clients, but as being strong in analytical skills. If so identified, usually
27 in their third or fourth year, they may be offered a position as a permanent associate. These people
28 are taken off the partnership track and are eventually compensated at about the rate of a sixth-year
29 associate.
30
31   Other associates are given a certain time within which to find alternative employment. Still
32 other associates leave voluntarily to other firms, to government or teaching positions, or because
33 they leave the area for personal reasons. Finally, some associates are identified as good potential
34 lawyers for the legal counsel offices of our clients. We will assist in placing them with our clients,
35 and usually they respond by continuing to send their business to P & G.
36
37   That's an outline of the procedures we follow. If you need a more complete outline, the best
38 person I know to talk to is Cliff Fuller. Cliff was my deputy chief of litigation and was intimately
39 involved in the evaluation process today. He is currently the Vice President and General Counsel of
40 one of my best clients, Nita Computer World (NCW) and has been so since April of 2002. He was
41 a partner in the firm for ten or eleven years before he left to join NCW. Cliff was one of my proteges
42 at the firm and is a very fine lawyer, having made partner in only six years.
43
44   As I said, I have been with P & G for approximately twenty-four years. I chose this firm over
45 others for a number of reasons. First, my wife's family has lived in Nita City for five generations and
46 it was her desire to live near her family. They are in the precision tool manufacturing business under
47 the business name of Preston Tools, Inc. Preston Tools is one of P & G's clients—has been for at

1 least fifty years. Amanda's grandfather and Herb Parker, one of the founders of P & G, were
2 apparently the best of friends. So, when looking for a law firm, I narrowed my search to the Nita
3 City area, and partially because of the family connection I applied to P & G. As luck would have it,
4 I received offers from five of the six largest firms in the city, and because P & G was willing to give
5 me partial credit for my time in the Justice Department towards a partnership decision while the
6 other firms were not, I decided to go with them. I have never regretted my decision. The firm has
7 grown nicely, and my personal litigation practice is varied and interesting, and over the years has
8 become national in scope.
9
10   To be honest, I am a very driven person. When I first started at P & G I was viewed by some
11 as having been hired to satisfy a good client of the firm. I became obsessed with my law practice and
12 put in enormous hours at the firm. As it turned out, that hard work has paid off professionally in that
13 I am now very well regarded. All that time and energy has taken its toll on my personal life. While
14 I focused on my law practice, my wife focused on the children and her various social and civic
15 activities, and over the years we have grown apart. To be honest, our marriage is one of convenience.
16 We have stayed together in name only and really have separate lives. The only time we spend any
17 appreciable time together is on the holidays and at family vacations. I'm sure that if it wasn't for the
18 children, we would have separated years ago, but because she makes no demands on me other than
19 whatever she gains socially from being married to a successful lawyer (she has inherited more
20 money than I'll ever have), we have remained together, at least in name. I'll admit there have been
21 times when I've considered asking her for a divorce, but each time Amanda has gotten very upset
22 and threatened to poison my already tenuous relationships with my children, so I've always backed
23 off. My children are very important to me, even though my practice, which often requires me to be
24 out of town for up to several months at a time has prevented me from developing a normal father-
25 child relationship with them.
26
27   I am aware of my reputation at P & G of being an office Lothario, and I suppose that, to some
28 extent, that it is deserved. Over the years I have had a number of sexual relationships with women
29 at the firm, including both paralegals and lawyers, but no where near the number put out by the firm
30 rumor mill. I have never, however, forced myself on anyone, nor used my position in the firm to
31 obtain sexual favors. Each relationship has been freely entered into by both myself and the woman
32 involved. In fact, in many circumstances the woman was the aggressor in the relationship.
33
34   These relationships normally evolve out of working long hours with the woman involved,
35 under the stress of litigation or trial. In those circumstances, much of which in my practice gets
36 played out in unfamiliar cities, there is a natural sexual tension that builds when two people work
37 closely together on a common goal. As a result the relationships, because they are born out of a
38 professional relationship involving a particular lawsuit, often end when the lawsuit that brought the
39 relationship about, ends. When I have been involved in these relationships, I am serious about them,
40 and they are monogamous. Because the woman involved often feels guilty about having an affair
41 with a married man, there is often talk of my getting a divorce. To be honest, in some of these
42 circumstances the relationship was, at the time, so satisfying that I truly believed that it might lead
43 to something permanent which would require a divorce. In other circumstances, I'll admit, that I
44 talked of divorce to please my partner or ease her conscience, but actually had no intention of leaving
45 Amanda.
46

1   When these relationships have ended, their termination has often times made the women
2   involved uncomfortable in the firm. In some cases their work performance has slipped, and for that
3   reason they have been let go. In other circumstances they have decided, that given my leadership
4   position in the firm, that they would be happier in another legal position and have left for that reason.
5   I have never, however, forced a woman with whom I've had a relationship out of P & G. I have no
6   reason to do so and I wouldn't consider such a thing. In addition, I have never done anything that
7   would hurt the professional opportunities at the firm of a woman with whom I have had a personal
8   relationship. Specifically, I have never asked my partners to reduce their requests for the legal
9   services of an associate, so as to lessen their billable hours, nor have I suggested that an associate's
10 work for me was of any quality other than it actually was, when I was asked for my evaluation as
11 a part of our regular evaluation process. In fact, when women with whom I have had a personal
12 relationship have chosen to leave the firm, I have done everything I could to assist them in finding
13 suitable other employment.
14
15   It is true that most of the women with whom I have had a personal relationship are no longer
16 with the firm, but that's true of most of the lawyers we hire as associates and most people we hire
17 as paralegals. Of the twenty litigation associates we hire in every given year, no more than three or
18 four will end up as a partner. Of those who end up as partners, approximately 25 percent will end
19 up leaving the firm to go to other firms or to start their own firms. As for paralegals, most of our
20 paralegals will only stay on with the firm for four or five years at the most. By that time, the good
21 ones usually go on to law school and end up practicing with entities other than P & G, and the ones
22 who are not so good are let go by the firm for inadequate work performance.
23
24   There is one woman, with whom I had a brief personal relationship who is a current partner
25 at P & G. I prefer not to divulge her identity, because she was married at the time of our relationship
26 and is still married to the same person.
27
28   I have had approximately ten extramarital relationships with women who were or are
29 employees of P & G. To be honest I cannot remember all of their names, given that the only such
30 relationship that I have had in the past six years has been the one with Maggie Polisi. If you can
31 suggest the names of women with who I am accused of having an affair, I will certainly confirm or
32 deny the fact, and tell you what I remember of the situation. I don't know anyone who might recall
33 their names except for Mary Langford, my longtime assistant, who makes all my travel arrangements
34 and handles my checking and credit card accounts.
35
36   I did have a relationship with a woman by the name of Susan McGinty, but that was easily
37 thirteen to fifteen years ago. She was an associate with the firm. The only reason I can time-frame
38 the relationship is because it was during a case involving most of the banks in Nita City and that
39 lasted for approximately two years. That case was the one in which I cemented my reputation with
40 the firm as a quality trial lawyer. Although I remember the case very well, I do not recall the
41 relationship with Ms. McGinty. I do know that she left the firm, but to be honest, I have no
42 recollection of the circumstances. I recall her to be a competent lawyer, but not someone who we had
43 earmarked for partnership.
44
45   I do recall a relationship with a paralegal by the name of Ellen Dorsen. That was about ten
46 to fifteen years ago. Ellen was a very aggressive young woman who worked with me on a case in
47 Memphis, Tennessee. She was a paralegal with the firm. The word on her among the male lawyers

1   was that she was only working at the firm in search of a husband. She was quite young, I believe
2   twenty-two or twenty-three. It was Ms. Dorsen who initiated the relationship, by coming to my hotel
3   room late one night, on the first trip on discovery that we made from Nita City to Memphis. She was
4   very attractive and given that I was substantially older than she—I was in my forties, I think—I was
5   flattered. Our relationship lasted the duration of that Memphis litigation. The word got back to me
6   that Ms. Dorsen was less than discrete about our relationship, actually flaunting it quite openly, and
7   that, together with the fact that I had tired of her, caused me to break off our relationship. No, I never
8   told Ms. Dorsen I would marry her or leave my wife for her; our relationship was a purely sexual
9   one. I know that Ms. Dorsen left the firm within a year of the ending of our relationship. I understand
10   she was let go for poor performance. I had no part in that decision, as those matters were handled
11   by our Paralegal's Committee. If I was contacted by the committee about my evaluation of her work,
12   I don't recall, but if I was I would have given my honest appraisal of her work, which was that it was
13   adequate.
14
15   I also recall a brief relationship with an associate by the name of Karen Newman. Our
16   relationship lasted about a month, which was the duration of a trial on which she assisted me in
17   Dallas, Texas. Using the case as a marker, that would make it about ten or eleven years ago. Ms.
18   Newman was a bright young woman. I believe that she was a mid-level associate at the time. The
19   relationship started after we had spent many hours working closely together on the preparation for,
20   and the trial of that case. One thing sort of led to another and we ended up as lovers. As I recall, it
21   was Karen who ended the relationship. She knew I was married, and although she was bright and
22   attractive, knew that I had no intention of leaving my wife for her, so she just ended the affair. I
23   don't know whether the subject of divorce ever came up with her; I just don't remember. I'll admit
24   that she might have bruised my male ego, but I certainly did not retaliate against her by damaging
25   her career in any way. As I recall, Ms. Newman left the firm about a year later and joined another
26   firm in Nita City. I know that I sent out, at her request, a very good letter of recommendation for her,
27   which I'm sure did not hurt her in obtaining another position. I am generally regarded, both in the
28   firm and in the community, as a good judge of legal talent. It is possible that Cliff Fuller might have
29   drafted that letter for me, but I just don't remember. He has done that sort of thing for me in the past.
30
31   I also recall a relationship with a young woman by the name of Carol Merritt. This
32   relationship was one which, at the time, I felt would lead to a more permanent situation. Ms. Merritt
33   was either a third- or fourth-year associate at the time of our relationship, which lasted for
34   approximately six months. She was very well regarded in the firm: bright, articulate, and talented.
35   As usual, the affair began because we were involved together in a lawsuit in which I was lead
36   counsel and to which she was assigned. The case was in Washington state and involved a lawsuit
37   by an environmental group to halt the cutting of trees in forests owned by our client. Using the case
38   as a time post, that must have been about ten years ago. At any rate, my relationship with Ms.
39   Merritt, began while we were in the final stages of discovery of that case, and lasted through the two-
40   and-a-half-month trial of the case and beyond.
41
42   Ms. Merritt was married at the time to her childhood sweetheart, and over time they had
43   apparently grown apart. Our relationship did not end, as was the usual pattern, with the case. We
44   were quite serious, and I truly believed at the time that I would get a divorce from my wife and
45   marry Carol, and I'm sure that she and I talked about my getting a divorce, because that was truly
46   my intention. She too, was quite serious, and eventually left her husband and took her own apartment
47   which I helped to finance. Our relationship lasted for about three months after the case ended. I

1 raised the issue of divorce with my wife on several occasions, but her threats of further distancing
2 me from my children eventually made me back down and I ended the relationship with Ms. Merritt.
3 Amanda also threatened to attempt to sour my business relationship with several of my clients who
4 were also social friends of hers and her family, but it was the threat to my relationships with my
5 children that caused me to back off my request for a divorce. Carol took the ending of the
6 relationship quite hard, and eventually took vacation and leave from the firm for approximately a
7 month before leaving the firm. She and her husband got their relationship back together, and moved
8 to Washington, D.C. I know that I sent out letters of recommendation on her behalf and that she
9 ended up with a very good firm there. Again the letters might have been drafted by Cliff Fuller, I just
10 don't recall. To be honest, I was the real loser in that situation in that our relationship was a good
11 one, much better than my relationship with my wife.
12
13   After my relationship with Carol Merritt, I don't believe I had another serious relationship
14 within the firm until the one with Maggie Polisi. There were several relationships with paralegals
15 over the next three years, but none of them were serious. I did not have a relationship with an
16 associate during that time, perhaps because of the difficulty with Ms. Merritt. As I said earlier, my
17 personal relationships never interfered with my professional judgment of an associate or a paralegal
18 and I never forced anyone out of the firm because of a failed personal relationship with me. As I
19 said, there is a current partner of the firm with whom I had a romantic relationship. No one else has
20 ever reached the partnership decision stage, usually at their own choosing. If they had, I would do
21 what I always do, and give an honest appraisal of the woman's legal ability.
22
23   In 1996, my son Spencer, who was then twelve years old, was involved in a serious accident
24 while he was riding his bicycle. He was quite severely injured and there was a period of time during
25 which there was some question about whether he was going to make it, although eventually he made
26 a full recovery. That experience actually brought Amanda and me together and it revived our
27 marriage. We remained close for several years, although we eventually grew apart again. During that
28 time, I had no extramarital affairs. As you know, I eventually got involved with Maggie Polisi, but
29 that was not until 2000.
30
31   Maggie Polisi started to work for P & G over fifteen years ago. The first real contact I had
32 with her was when she worked with me as a paralegal in the bank litigation case I spoke of earlier
33 in 1988 through 1990. As I said, this was a very important and complicated case, and her work was
34 exemplary. Ms. Polisi was eventually selected to work as one of the trial paralegals in the case and
35 did a fine job for me. I was very impressed with her work, as was Cliff Fuller, who was one of the
36 associates who worked closely with me on that case. At the end of that case, I remember
37 complimenting Ms. Polisi on her work and suggesting that she go to law school. Although it was my
38 recommendation that she go full time, she was a single mother and needed to work while in law
39 school. As a result she went to Nita University School of Law as a night student.
40
41   During Ms. Polisi's time in law school, she continued to work at the firm and from time to
42 time she did work for me. Because I considered her to have a good deal of natural talent, and because
43 I liked her personally, I kept tabs on her law school career. As it turned out, she did very well in law
44 school, while at the same time performing top-notch work, first as a paralegal, and then as a law
45 clerk at the firm. I might have checked on her progress with her from time to time, and now that you
46 ask, I believe that I took her out to lunch once or twice to celebrate her successes at school. I had no
47 interest in her, other than professional at that time. I might have commented that she looked

1   attractive from time to time, or flirted with her. That is just the way I am. I am also a very physical
2   person. It is not uncommon for me to touch the person with whom I'm speaking while doing so, both
3   male and female. I might have done this with Maggie Polisi, but I certainly didn't mean anything
4   by it, and I have no recollection of doing so. As I said I had no personal interest in her at that time.
5
6   I do recall that I did go to bat for her during her first year as a law clerk. Law clerks do not
7   receive bonuses at P & G. That is because the firm generally does not have any long-term interest
8   in them, unlike the good paralegals and associates. Because Ms. Polisi had been a paralegal, and
9   because I guess in the back of my mind I saw her as a potential associate, I argued with the then-
10 chief of litigation that she should remain eligible for bonuses. He went along and I gave her a bonus
11 check whatever the first year of her working as an associate would have been. I remember that she
12 was quite excited to receive it, and was very grateful.
13
14   During Ms. Polisi's four years in law school, she did some work for me, all of it very high
15 quality. I would have asked for her on more of my cases except for the fact that, because of her
16 situation as a single parent, she did not travel for extended periods of time, and most of my cases
17 were out of town. At any rate, her work was always first-rate for me, and I was told by Cliff Fuller,
18 for whom she apparently did quite a bit of work, that her work as a law clerk was better than that of
19 some of our associates.
20
21   In 1993, I was the chair of the hiring committee for the law firm, and one of its most active
22 members was Cliff Fuller. Cliff approached me in the fall of 1993 about the potential of hiring
23 Maggie Polisi as an associate of the firm. I pointed out to him that such a move was unprecedented
24 in that we had never, up until that point, hired a law clerk as an associate. It was also true at that time
25 that we had never hired a graduate of the evening division of Nita University School of Law as an
26 associate. Those two facts went together, as most of our regular full-time law clerks are students at
27 Nita U. in the evening division. Cliff argued that Maggie's work was first-rate, that there was no
28 difference in the education at Nita U. between the day and the evening division, and finally, that our
29 summer associates for 1993 had not been a particularly impressive group. It was and is our habit to
30 hire most of our associates out of the Summer Associates Program, but that particular year, I had to
31 agree with Cliff, that we were less impressed with the group than normal.
32
33   I agreed with Cliff to quietly ask the hiring committee for its opinion on the prospect of
34 hiring Maggie Polisi, and although there were some opposed, most agreed that she could be
35 interviewed. As a result Cliff and I approached Maggie and encouraged her to apply. We made it
36 clear, however, that it was not certain that she would receive an offer, but that she would get a fair
37 look and both of us would support her. She seemed quite flattered and excited at the prospect. She
38 eventually did apply and go through the interviewing process. There was some opposition, primarily
39 based on the fact that she was an evening division student and a law clerk. The only other negative
40 to her coming on board was her need, due to her responsibilities as a single mother, to be assigned
41 to cases that kept her predominantly in Nita City. As I've said, our practice is national in scope and
42 our associates are often times required to set up shop in the city where the case is being litigated.
43 Maggie's inability to do so presented the most substantive roadblock to her receiving an offer. The
44 most vociferous opponent to our hiring her was Jayne Post, who is and was a partner in the litigation
45 section of the firm. In the end we felt the positives outweighed any negative and an offer was
46 authorized. I was the person who conveyed our offer and she accepted immediately. She seemed
47 quite pleased and excited to come to work at P & G.

1   For Ms. Polisi's first five years at the firm as an associate, she did very little work for me.
2   That was predominantly because most of my practice requires the associates assigned to my cases
3   to travel out of town. What work she did do for me was first-rate and seemed to justify our offer to
4   her. She did do a great deal of work for Cliff Fuller, however, and he was most complimentary of
5   her abilities. I believe that she was graded at the C level for her first year, which is a fairly typical
6   grade. She received B's in her second, third and fourth years. These grades are quite good and as of
7   her fourth year she was considered a very good candidate for a partnership. There were some
8   lingering questions about her law school, and her inability to travel, but she was actually doing quite
9   well. There were also some questions about her toughness and aggressiveness.
10
11   In 1999, Ms. Polisi's fifth with the firm, she had a horrible year. There were some serious
12   negative comments about the quality of her work and her billable hours were down substantially.
13   Those two factors often go hand in hand. If there are problems with an associate's work, they will
14   be requested less often by partners in need of staffing for their cases. As a result, the billable hours
15   will go down. I was told by Cliff Fuller that Maggie lost her father after a two month illness, which
16   required her out to be of town on a regular basis, and that in addition, her teenage children had also
17   had rough years, as teenagers often do, and that these events coincided to explain Maggie's poor
18   performance. Because by that time I had become the chief of the litigation section, I heard the
19   complaints about Maggie's work personally, as did Cliff Fuller, who I had selected to be my deputy.
20
21   Q: What grade did Ms. Polisi receive for her fifth year?
22
23   A: Because I was an admirer of Maggie Polisi, and at Cliff's request, I did the best I could
24   during the evaluation of Maggie, but the highest grade we could justify was a C.
25
26   Q: What usually happens to an associate's career at P & G if they receive a C grade in their fifth
27   year?
28
29   A: A grade of C in the fifth year of an associate's career usually spells the end of his association
30   with the firm. Sometimes we will assist in finding a job for the associate with a client, but
31   usually the associate is given a good recommendation and finds a new position on their own.
32
33   Q: Did that happen in Ms. Polisi's case?
34
35   A: No. At my insistence, my partners approved a third alternative for her. I was about to enter
36   into a fast-tracked litigation on behalf of Nita Computer World in which they were alleged to
37   have participated in a price fixing scheme with other retailers of computers hardware and
38   software, and I needed a senior associate on the case. My partners agreed that if I was willing
39   to take the risk, that they should as well.
40
41   Cliff and I presented the evaluation to Maggie and gave her the alternatives I just mentioned.
42   As we expected, she chose to sign onto the NCW case even though I made it clear that there was
43   some substantial travel involved in the case. As it turned out, our faith in Maggie was well placed,
44   given her performance on the NCW case. She, quite frankly, did a superb job and her work was so
45   recognized not only by me, but by the two other partners on the case. In fact, her advocacy on an
46   important protective order that we sought to protect from discovery some of NCW's trade secrets,

1   was so effective that she was complimented individually in a letter from NCW's General Counsel.
2   (SEE EXHIBIT 6)
3
4   During the NCW case, which ran non-stop from late September of 1999 through June of 2000,
5   Maggie and I were in constant contact. She often times traveled with me or one of the other partners
6   when motions were argued or for depositions. She also conducted a number of depositions herself.
7   Maggie was also present for all of the strategy and case theory sessions. As the case heated up, it was
8   not unusual for depositions to be scheduled in clusters and Maggie would often times participate in
9   the prep sessions that usually were held in my suite. When the work for the day was over, we often
10 ordered a late meal or some wine to unwind and relax. This occurred with other members of the
11 litigation team present, although sometimes we were alone. Over the course of the litigation we
12 became closer, talking often about personal matters. She told me all about her marriage and family
13 and I did the same. There was no sexual relationship, although I'll admit that I was attracted to her,
14 but we did develop a close personal relationship. She did send some signals that she was interested
15 in a physical relationship by the way she looked, or by the touch of her hand, but although my wife
16 and I were back to our separate lives, nothing came of it. I do not recall making any sexual advances
17 towards her during the time of the litigation.
18
19   When the case settled on extremely favorable terms to NCW in June of 2000, the client
20 thanked the litigation team by sending us on a week's vacation to the Bahamas. Spouses were
21 invited, but neither Maggie nor I brought anyone along. It was during this vacation that we became
22 physically intimate. I don't think either one of us intended it to happen, it just seemed like the natural
23 progression in our relationship. It was in this way that the beginning of my relationship with Maggie
24 Polisi was different than others that I had with women at the firm. In all of the other relationships,
25 the physical relationship was first, followed in some cases, such as with Carol Merritt, by a more
26 meaningful relationship. With Maggie Polisi, the relationship just evolved naturally.
27
28   I was convinced that Maggie and I would eventually be married, and we started to make
29 plans for our lives together. We spent a great deal of time together and everything seemed to be
30 working out well. I told her that I wanted to wait to file for divorce until my son, Spencer, was
31 enrolled in college and away from home. When he had a hard time adjusting to college I later put
32 that time off until the end of the first semester. Maggie was very understanding about my concern
33 for Spencer initially, but in the end she just couldn't wait. She also became very upset when I went
34 to a family gathering on Labor Day of 2000, where I saw my first grandchild for the first time, and
35 when I insisted on spending what I thought would be my last family gathering over the holidays in
36 December of 2000 and January of 2001. It was my plan at that time to tell Amanda that I was filing
37 for divorce, but when it became apparent that Spencer was not doing very well in his transition to
38 college, I determined that in his interest, I should wait until the end of the first year.
39
40   In the end, Maggie just could not be patient, and gave me an ultimatum in January of 2001
41 to file for divorce or end our relationship. Because of my son, I just wasn't able to do it, so I lost her.
42 It was Maggie who made the decision to part, not me. Fortunately, I had a case that took me away
43 for several months and the work let me heal my wounds. When the relationship ended I was hurt,
44 but I never made any threats to her professional career at P & G and never did anything that was
45 intended to harm her and her position at the firm. I do not recall any conversation specifically with
46 Maggie on the day she ended our relationship. I certainly never threatened her, either personally or
47 with regard to her employment at the firm. I do remember offering to take her on a trip, but she

1 turned me down. In March of 2001, when I returned from my case, I did call and ask Maggie out to
2 dinner, but she declined.
3
4   I understand that Maggie had some difficulty as well, in that she had some health problems
5 that caused her to be out of the office, and, in addition, the quality of her work slipped. In a law firm,
6 when an associate starts to produce poorly, especially a senior associate, it is hard for them to get
7 work, so I'm not surprised that her billable hours started to fall back. This is a shame because based
8 on her work on the NCW case, Maggie had been graded at the A level for her sixth year and seemed
9 on track to be made partner in June of 2001. This is especially so in that after the NCW case she
10 continued to perform at a very high level until the winter and spring of 2001.
11
12   I certainly had nothing to do with the drop-off in Maggie's work. That was a result of her
13 performance, and to suggest that I had anything to do with it is ridiculous. If anything, because I was
14 so effusive (and rightfully so on the merits) about Maggie's performance on the NCW case, she
15 received more than her share of quality assignments in 2000. That they did not continue is her own
16 doing.
17
18   The drop-off in work was certainly apparent when Cliff Fuller started to prepare an
19 evaluation for the meeting on partnership by the litigation section in June of 2001. Because of my
20 relationship with Maggie, I thought it best that Cliff take charge of the evaluation. As a result, and
21 after consultation with me, he suggested to Maggie that she put off her partnership decision until
22 2002, so that she could repair her reputation which had been damaged by her poor (for her) quality
23 work. In the end she did not take our advice and even though I spoke in her favor, she was not
24 nominated for partnership. Because our relationship was common knowledge within the firm, I
25 decided to abstain in the vote, but that abstention had no effect on the outcome, because, as chair,
26 I only voted in the case of a tie, and there was not a tie vote on her candidacy. She may have asked
27 to be reconsidered in a year, but the partnership decision was final. The issue of non-equity
28 partnership for Ms. Polisi was never raised as it would not have made a difference in this case.
29
30   At the meeting, the primary concern was how Maggie responded to personal difficulties. Our
31 clients have the right to expect high quality lawyering from us, no matter what else is happening in
32 our lives. Maggie, within three years, had shown two times when she wasn't able to put aside
33 personal problems and remain focused on her work. In the end, that is what, in my opinion, killed
34 her candidacy. As is typical in these situations, Maggie was given a six-month grace period to find
35 another position. I always thought that she would go on and be successful in law practice, although
36 I understand that she had a hard time finding another position with a law firm. I did write and send
37 out a number of recommendation letters on her behalf when requested to do so by potential
38 employers. (SEE EXHIBITS 11, 12, 13) I did not send out the letter drafted for me by Cliff Fuller.
39 (SEE EXHIBIT 10) In all honesty I thought the letter was too effusive and therefore not an accurate
40 reflection of my opinion of Maggie's abilities. So I drafted my own letter. I also knew at that time
41 that Maggie had complained to the EEOC and thought that it would not be a good idea to have an
42 overly effusive letter that could later be used against us in some legal preceding.
43
44   I have looked at Exhibit 11 and can identify the first handwritten note on the bottom of the
45 letter as my own. The second notation is not in my handwriting. John Randall is an old and close
46 friend. His practice is predominantly a white-collar-criminal defense practice. Our practice at P &
47 G is all civil but tends to involve the same kinds of transactions that sometimes find their way into

1 criminal court. For that reason I thought that Maggie's resume might be attractive to him. On the
2 other hand, his practice is much more pressurized and fast-paced than ours, and given Maggie's
3 history at the firm of having trouble separating personal crises from professional performance, I did
4 not think that she was a good fit. I don't recall if I spoke to John Randall on the phone, but if I did,
5 I'm sure I said to him what I just said to you about Maggie's fit with that firm. Looking at Exhibits
6 8 and 9 I can identify them as my phone logs for the dates shown. The check marks are mine. They
7 mean that I returned the calls checked off. They do not mean that I ever actually spoke to the people
8 I called back. I do not recall speaking to anyone else about Maggie Polisi, by way of giving her a
9 reference. I might have; I just don't recall.
10
11   My not using Cliff's draft of a recommendation letter for Maggie did cause me some
12 problems with Cliff. He came in to talk to me about it sometime in early 2002. Apparently he had
13 represented to Maggie that I would send out the letter he had drafted. I told him what I told you
14 about why I had written my own letter. It was my attempt to give an honest appraisal of Maggie's
15 abilities, and not in any way an attempt to do her any harm.
16
17   As it turned out, Maggie decided on a teaching career, and is now on the faculty at the
18 University of Nita School of Law. I sent a letter on her behalf to the Dean of the law school, Marty
19 Purcell, who was a law school classmate of mine at Harvard. The letter may have been a form of the
20 letter drafted for me by Cliff Fuller. It is different from the letter I sent to the law firms back in 2001,
21 mainly because the job requirements are different. I truly believe that Maggie will flourish in the
22 more sheltered environment of academia.
23
24   The others in Maggie's class who came up for partnership in 2001, Mark Hancock and Roger
25 Kramer, were easy choices. Mark had distinguished himself in the courtroom during an important
26 trial in the spring of 2001 and the client made it clear that Mark should be assigned to their trial
27 cases. Roger had been the most solid performer in that class, and was also the son of the president
28 of one of our best clients. Mike DeAngelo was put off for a year to see if he could improve his
29 performance in the area of client relations. He ended up having a good year, and attracted a new
30 client to the firm, and was granted partnership in June of 2002. Although it might appear that Mike
31 and Maggie were treated differently, in that Mike was allowed another year to improve, the cases
32 are really different. Mike had been a rock-solid, consistent performer and we were just looking for
33 a little spark to push him over the edge. Maggie had shown brilliance and real lows, and another year
34 would not dispel the concern that her work would suffer every time she encountered a personal
35 problem.
36
37   I know that Cliff Fuller believes that I am responsible for Maggie's not making partner. In
38 reality, however, I did nothing to hurt her chances; it was all her own doing. I never did or said
39 anything that was intended to harm her work assignments or the way she was thought of in the firm.
40 Most of what occurred that hurt her actually happened while I was out of town. I know that Cliff is
41 particularly angry with me, but he has always been overly involved in the promotion of Maggie
42 Polisi within the firm, and he is just disappointed. I assume that he'll get over it in time. We have
43 maintained a good professional relationship since he has moved over to NCW. He is my contact at
44 NCW, and has corporate responsibility for overseeing P & G's performance on litigation matters we
45 handle for them.
46

1   In September of 2001, I stepped down as the chief of the litigation section. Although the
2 normal term in five years and I had not completed my term, I thought that I was out of town on my
3 own cases too frequently to do a good job of administering the section, so Rob Bryant took over. To
4 maintain continuity, Cliff Fuller stayed on as his deputy until he left P & G in 2002. In no way was
5 my relationship with Maggie Polisi causative of my leaving the position.
6
7   As I mentioned earlier, we received notification from the EEOC that a complaint had been
8 filed against us by Ms. Polisi in the summer of 2001. (SEE EXHIBIT 14) I was consulted about our
9 response and Rob Bryant responded with a general denial. (SEE EXHIBIT 15) We received
10 notification from the EEOC in December of 2001 that they had issued a "right to sue" letter to her
11 so the filing of this lawsuit is not surprising. (SEE EXHIBIT 16) It is, however, in my opinion not
12 well taken at all. No decision at P & G regarding Ms. Polisi was ever motivated by a sexually
13 discriminatory act. She just failed to make the grade, on the merits. I'm sorry it turned out that way,
14 but it did.

      I have read this deposition and it is complete and accurate.

Simon Clark

Simon Clark

      Subscribed and sworn before me this 20th day of December, 2002.

Harry Gibbons

Harry Gibbons CSR
Certified Shorthand Reporter

      This deposition was given under oath at the offices of plaintiff's counsel on November 27, 2002. This deposition was given under oath, read and signed by the deponent.

DEPOSITION OF JAYNE POST

1   My name is Jayne Post. I am forty-six years old and a partner in the law firm of Parker &
2   Gould (P & G). I am married to Harvey Wilkes and we live at 25 Woodcrest Place in Nita City.
3   Harvey owns a small construction business in Nita City. We do not have any children. Our careers
4   didn't leave time to properly raise children, so we decided against becoming parents.
5

6   I graduated from Yale University in 1979 with a BA degree in English. I graduated with
7   honors from Yale and three years later, in 1982, graduated from Cornell Law School, where I was
8   an honors graduate and an editor of the Cornell Law Review. That same year I became an associate
9   at Parker & Gould. At that time I was one of two women in the litigation section of the firm that had
10 about forty lawyers, fifteen or whom were partners. There were no women partners in the litigation
11 section when I started with the firm. In fact there were only three women partners in the firm which
12 had approximately 100 lawyers, two in the corporate section and one in the tax section. At that time
13 there were no women partners in the estates section of the firm. When I was made a partner in the
14 firm in 1990, I was the first woman partner in the litigation section. The firm now has six women
15 partners in the litigation section of about thirty-five partners. Sherry Barker, Ann Feinman, and
16 Georgia Bratton work with me in my domestic relations sub-group. They became partners in 1993,
17 1996, and 2000 respectively. Cheryl Stein and Kathryn Kowalski are also partners and work with
18 John Crandall in his bankruptcy sub-group. They became partners in 1997 and 2000 respectively.
19

20   P & G does not have the longest history of treating women fairly in hiring and partnership
21 decisions, but I'd say in the thirteen years that I have been a partner that women have received equal
22 opportunities in the firm. Since I have been a partner, I have made sure of that. This is true for a
23 variety of reasons. First, the main opposition to women lawyers in the firm had apparently come
24 from some of the partners who were most senior when I joined the firm. These people have since
25 retired or have been silenced by the majority in the firm. Second, women are now graduating from
26 law school at about the same rate as men (unlike when I was in law school), and if the firm wants
27 the most-talented lawyers, it's necessary to hire women. At P & G, talent is the most important
28 quality for a lawyer, so we have, for at least the last five years, been hiring about the same number
29 of men and women in our associates classes.
30

31   Women are also working their way through the firm to partnership and in 2000, two women,
32 Georgia Bratton and Kathryn Kowlaski, were made partner in the litigation section, while only one
33 man, Dave Hamilton, made the grade. All partners in the firm are equity partners. We have
34 considered granting non-equity partnerships in cases where the candidate is highly qualified but
35 lacks the ability to attract or keep clients. That eventually has not yet occurred, although I am sure
36 it will in the future.
37

38   I'll admit that when I was coming through the firm that it was a struggle for a woman. The
39 partners were initially unwilling to try to work with a woman lawyer, just because they weren't used
40 to it. I had to fight to get good assignments in order to get recognized within the firm, and even when
41 I did a good job, it never seemed to be enough. During my evaluations I constantly received
42 comments that questioned my aggressiveness, although no one could give any examples of my not
43 being aggressive enough. It was a tough struggle, but eventually I was recognized for the talent that
44 I had. The main thing in my favor, I think, was that my billable hours were always first or second

1	in my associates class. I was also willing to travel anywhere, at any time, and never turned down an
2	assignment, no matter how pushed I was. Fortunately for me, my husband was very understanding
3	and he stuck with me over the years. Although it took eight, as opposed to the then-normal seven,
4	years to make partner, I hung on and worked extremely hard and made the grade as the first woman
5	partner in the litigation section.
6
7	 There were two things in the final analysis, that got me over the partnership hump. First, I
8	worked on a case with Simon Clark in 1987, and he was very complimentary of my work to his
9	partners. Simon was, at the time, a rising star in the firm (he was in his late thirties then) and his
10	comments to his partners helped in my getting some good assignments where I could show my
11	abilities. I also know that Simon persuaded his partners to give me an extra year to make partner and
12	spoke very highly of my abilities during the litigation section partnership meeting during which I
13	was nominated for partnership. Second, although it started as a reflection of my apparent second-
14	class citizenship in the firm, my willingness to work on and succeed in domestic relations matters
15	for the officers of several of our best corporate clients gained me respect by the clients, which
16	translated into respect in the firm. I also enjoyed the work and the independence it gave me within
17	the firm. Because the work was not mainline litigation, most of the partners did not want to become
18	involved in it, so I had a great deal of autonomy, wherein I could showcase my abilities.
19
20	 It was for that reason that once I made partner, that even though I was entitled to work in
21	general litigation, I persuaded my partners in the litigation section to allow me to try to build a
22	domestic relations practice within the firm. Although initially reluctant, they finally agreed and I
23	now have a thriving practice. There are now four partners in my sub-group, including myself, and
24	we have about six or so associates working with us. All of the partners are women. This is more by
25	happenstance than by design. Because I made it a point to give our women associates plenty of work
26	when they needed it, and involved them in the full range of litigation when some of my partners
27	would not, there was a natural gravitation by some women to my sub-group. In addition, I have
28	actively promoted women within the firm and served as a mentor for many of them. The associates
29	who now work with us are about evenly split between men and women, and I expect that within a
30	few years, one of the men will be made a partner in the firm and continue to work in my sub-group.
31
32	 I think that I have the respect of my partners, but I know that there remains some elitism
33	concerning the various sorts of practice within the litigation section. Both domestic relations and
34	John Crandall's bankruptcy sub-group suffer from a similar prejudice with the section. Because our
35	practices are specialized, some members of the firm view it as somehow less demanding than the
36	run-of-the-mill commercial litigation within the firm. For that reason, I have always counseled the
37	women associates within the firm to work to get a well-rounded selection of cases to work on in the
38	firm, so that they can showcase their talents. That is so even if they would prefer to specialize in
39	either domestic relations or bankruptcy. This is the kind of advice that associates need to hear at P
40	& G and I have made sure over the years that the women associates have gotten the same kind of
41	good advice that the men, with their mentors, got when I was coming up through the ranks.
42
43	 The associates at the firm in the litigation section are evaluated each year. The process
44	requires the section chief and deputy section chief to interview all the partners for whom the
45	associate has done work during the year, solicit comments from the rest of the firm members, review
46	the associate's billable hours, and with all this information come up with an evaluation grade from
47	A–F. The grade, and the basis for the grade, is then reviewed with the associate, so that they can

1   either improve or choose to move on to another firm or another position within the profession. Part
2   of the process is to inform the associate how many other associates in their class got the same grade,
3   and how many did better, so they can rank themselves within their class. Exhibits 3A–3G, and
4   Exhibits 5A–5H, the evaluation memos concerning Margaret Polisi and Michael DeAngelo are
5   typical examples of the form, and basically reflect the kind of information that is provided by the
6   firm to our associates by way of evaluation.
7
8   During the associate's first four years, the typical grade is C, with those people who achieve
9   B's on a regular basis usually making up the top three or four people within each class. At the fourth
10 year, some associates are told to seek other employment, some are assisted in finding jobs with one
11 of our clients (which promotes good relations with the former associate and the client) and some
12 associates, who are intellectually able but lacking in the people skills necessary to make partner, are
13 offered jobs as permanent associates who usually earn about the same salary as sixth-year associates,
14 but have no possibility of ever becoming a partner. The fifth and sixth years are important for those
15 associates who will make partner, in that during those years they must show themselves to be
16 special. It is during those years that the associate should usually be graded at the A level if they
17 expect to be made partner.
18
19   The partnership decision is normally made during June of the associate's seventh year, but
20 can be put over to the eighth year. At that time, the litigation section partners vote on whether to
21 nominate the associate for partnership. The associate must receive a majority vote of the partners in
22 the section. If we choose not to, in unusual circumstances the associate may be given another year
23 to show his or her abilities, but usually the associate is given six months in which to find another
24 position. If the associate is nominated for partnership, his or her name is sent to the firm's Executive
25 Committee, which then presents the associate to the entire partnership. I know of no time since I've
26 been with the firm, that the firm's Executive Committee has failed to present the nominee of one of
27 the litigation section's associates to the entire partnership. The same is true for the nominees from
28 the other three sections of the firm: corporate, tax, and estates. The nominee must then receive a
29 majority vote from the entire partnership. The partnership will consider the evaluation grades of the
30 associates, giving additional positive consideration to an associate who has demonstrated the ability
31 to attract business to the firm.
32
33   As I said earlier, Simon Clark was instrumental in getting his partners to give me a fair shot
34 at P & G and for that I will be forever grateful. He evaluated me on my ability and not my gender,
35 when others were not willing to do so. He is, as I'm sure you know, the top litigator and trial lawyer
36 in the litigation section at P & G. He is also very active in pro bono work for the Nita chapter of the
37 ACLU. Because of his abilities, he is also responsible for attracting and keeping many of the major
38 clients of the firm. I respect him as a lawyer, but he does have a fatal flaw.
39
40   Simon Clark has, from what I have picked up over the years, a well-deserved reputation as
41 a womanizer. He is apparently married in name only and he and his wife must have an understanding
42 of some sort, because during my time with the firm he has had several well-publicized affairs with
43 either paralegals or associates in the firm, and there are rumors of many more such affairs. To be
44 honest, it is the source of some embarrassment to the firm that his behavior has been tolerated over
45 the years, and it probably would not have been, but for his extraordinary legal ability.
46

1   Although I know none of the details, I am aware that during a period of three of four years
2   about ten to fifteen years ago that he had rather public relationships with a paralegal by the name of
3   Ellen Dorsen, and associates by the names of Karen Newman, Susan McGinty, and Carol Merritt.
4   None of these women are still with the firm. Of the four, I know that Karen Newman is a lawyer here
5   in Nita City. I have no information about any of the others. I don't know the circumstances under
6   which they left the firm, as I wasn't particularly close to any of those women, but given Simon's
7   position of prominence in the firm, even back then, and the fact that they were in lesser positions,
8   I can only assume that they figured out that it would be more comfortable for them to be somewhere
9   else.
10
11   I don't believe that they were forced to leave. The firm would never be involved in any
12 activity of that sort, but in such a situation, if the firm had to choose at some point between an
13 extremely talented and productive partner and an unproven associate, the business decision would
14 seem obvious to me. That's not discrimination; that's just business. Fortunately, we have never had
15 to make such a stark decision, although in the case of Maggie Polisi, some of my partners might have
16 viewed the partnership decision on her in that manner. If they did so, they were making a decision
17 on a purely business basis, but I think that her being denied partnership was an appropriate decision
18 on the merits.
19
20   Ms. Polisi started to work for P & G as a paralegal. I don't know the date with precision, but
21 believe that it was over fifteen years ago. At some point she decided to go to law school, and during
22 that time continued to work as a paralegal and then a law clerk at the firm. This was possible because
23 she attended the University of Nita School of Law as an evening division student. In 1993, I was one
24 of the members of the hiring committee that was chaired by Simon Clark. Another partner on the
25 committee was Cliff Fuller. At that time, Cliff was a new partner in the firm, having received a
26 partnership offer in his sixth year as an associate, a year before anyone else in his class. Cliff was
27 an extraordinarily bright graduate of the University of Nita School of Law (our first partner from that
28 school) and the protege of Simon Clark.
29
30   It was Simon Clark and Cliff Fuller who put Ms. Polisi's name forward as a potential
31 associate. At that point no law clerk from the firm had ever been made an offer to become an
32 associate. This policy was a good one, I think, because it kept the law clerks focused on their work,
33 and not advancing their careers by making political connections within the firm. In addition, we had
34 never made an offer to a graduate of the evening division of Nita University School of Law. There
35 was some feeling within the firm that the evening division program was less rigorous than the
36 regular three-year program, and although by that point we had our first partner (Cliff) and several
37 associates who were graduates of the day division of that school, we had never hired anyone form
38 the evening division. Personally, I had no information about the difference, if any, between the full-
39 time and part-time program, but did feel that the full-time study of law, free from the distractions
40 of work, was a better way to learn the law, but that's probably because that's the way I went to
41 school.
42
43   Simon Clark approached me personally about hiring Ms. Polisi. I'll have to say, that because
44 of the problem with violating our unwritten policy, I was initially opposed. Simon persuaded me that
45 there was no harm in interviewing her and said that she had done some good work for him, and that
46 Cliff was particularly impressed with her. I therefore reluctantly agreed to her going through the
47 process.

1   I'll have to admit that Ms. Polisi was very impressive in her interview. I also got to review
2 some of her written work as a law clerk (she had never done any work for me) and it demonstrated
3 excellent research and analysis skills, even though the writing style was a little wordy, a not
4 uncommon ailment for most of our associates. Her grades were also excellent and as it turned out
5 she graduated magna cum laude and first in her class. In the end, despite her qualifications, I was not
6 positive on her appointment. The turning point for me was that although she was interested in
7 working in general commercial litigation, Ms. Polisi was adamant about not being sent out of Nita
8 City on assignment for extended periods of time. This was because she was the single parent of two
9 children. While I was sympathetic to her request, I thought it was unfair to the other associates in
10 her class, and really unfair to the firm.
11
12   The other associates in the firm would have to bear the burden of the out-of-town work that
13 would normally be hers. The firm would be deprived from the ability to evaluate her performance
14 under the stress of working in unfamiliar work environments where much of our practice occurs. P
15 & G has a national litigation practice. We will litigate cases wherever our clients do business. As a
16 result, Ms. Polisi's limitations on travel made it impossible for the firm to get a complete reading
17 on how she would likely perform as a general litigation partner.
18
19   In the end, however, my arguments did not prevail. Cliff Fuller, and to a lesser extent Simon
20 Clark, were very positive towards her appointment and their opinion carried the day. They were
21 probably successful, at least in part, because our summer associates' class from 1993, from which
22 we normally would draw most of our associates, was not very strong for some reason, and so Ms.
23 Polisi's application was probably viewed more favorably than it would have been in a more normal
24 year.
25
26   As it turned out Ms. Polisi's first four years at the firm went very well. She was graded at the
27 B level for at least three of those years and appeared to be doing a good job. She did very little work
28 for me, but when she did it was good. She was by far not the best associate to work for me in her
29 class, but her work was acceptable and she seemed to respond well to comments that I made on her
30 work for me. Cliff Fuller was apparently acting as her mentor and he seemed to guide her to some
31 of the larger cases for our bigger clients, which, according to the conventional wisdom at P & G, was
32 the best way for an associate to get a good reputation within the firm. I continued, during that time,
33 to question whether it was appropriate for an associate to get a free ride on the demanding out-of-
34 town practice that was required of our general litigation associates, but to no avail. It seemed to me
35 that Ms. Polisi's children, who were then teenagers, were old enough to be left for extended periods
36 of time with hired child-care professionals. After all, associates were normally not out of town more
37 that four nights a week, as usually they would fly home on Friday evenings, and back out on Monday
38 mornings. This was the routine when I was an associate and remains the routine today. At any rate,
39 given her evaluations, my qualms aside, and with the active support and guidance of Cliff Fuller, Ms.
40 Polisi seemed to be on track to a partnership.
41
42   That changed in her fifth year, which ended in 1999. For personal reasons that I've never
43 been clear of, except to the extent that I think it involved the death of a parent or some problems with
44 her children, Ms. Polisi's work fell off dramatically. There were real questions expressed about the
45 quality of her work and her billable hours were down significantly. She was ultimately evaluated at
46 the C level, which normally would call for the firm giving her a certain time in which to find
47 alternative employment. And that's what would have happened but for the intervention of Simon

1   Clark, who by that time had been named the chief of the litigation section. Simon persuaded the
2   partners in the litigation section to allow him to present several alternatives to Ms. Polisi: first, to
3   seek other employment; second, to make a recommendation, that would undoubtedly be accepted
4   by the client, that she take a job with the general counsel's office of Nita Computer World (NCW),
5   one of Simon's good clients; or third, to work on a very complicated and fast-tracked litigation on
6   behalf of NCW with Simon Clark and his team, to see if she could make up for her bad year.
7   Although there was some opposition in the section, we went along with Simon's recommendation
8   and the alternatives were presented to Ms. Polisi. She opted for working on the NCW case.
9
10   As it turned out, her decision was a good one for her, because according to Simon and the
11 other partners who worked on the case to a very successful conclusion, her work on the case was
12 exemplary. I have also seen a letter from NCW that singles her out for praise on the work she did
13 on the case. (SEE EXHIBIT 6) Based in part on that performance, she received very good
14 assignments from other partners, and continued to work at a high level. As a result, Ms. Polisi was
15 graded at the A level for her sixth year and seemed to be positioned to make partner in June of 2001.
16
17   Unfortunately for Ms. Polisi, she also began a personal relationship with Simon Clark. The
18 rumors about Simon had subsided during the several years before the NCW case, so I was surprised
19 when I heard about the relationship. There was no doubt, however, that she was involved with Simon
20 and the rumors were that Simon was going to divorce his wife and marry Ms. Polisi.
21
22   The personal relationship between Ms. Polisi and Simon Clark made me wonder about the
23 validity of her performance evaluation. That is, I was concerned that Simon was not evaluating her
24 solely on job performance, and that others of my partners were giving good references to please
25 Simon as opposed to on the merits. I therefore requested that Ms. Polisi be assigned to a complicated
26 distribution of assets case I had that involved the division of several corporations. I thought that this
27 case would demonstrate Ms. Polisi's abilities, and therefore, that I could be comfortable in voting
28 for her partnership. My request for her assistance was turned down, however, because she was
29 working with Cliff Fuller on another matter for NCW at the same I time I needed her, so she never
30 worked for me.
31
32   In January of 2001, the relationship between Simon Clark and Ms. Polisi apparently ended.
33 For that or other personal reasons, Ms. Polisi's work leading up to the partnership decision date in
34 June of 2001, again dropped off in terms of quality and quantity. I know that Cliff Fuller counseled
35 Ms. Polisi to put off her going forward for partner for a year, but she refused to do so. As a result,
36 we had a rather rancorous meeting in considering whether the litigation section should nominate her
37 for partnership.
38
39   In the end, it was the concern of partners that Ms. Polisi was unable to separate her personal
40 life from her professional life that caused her not to be nominated. The argument that carried the day
41 was that in two of the three years leading up to the partnership decision, the existence of a personal
42 problem caused Ms. Polisi's work to drop off, and that behavior cannot be tolerated by P & G
43 partners, who have the responsibility for high-quality representation of our clients with very little
44 intervening guidance from other lawyers in the firm. We felt that her candidacy was just too risky.
45 There was also some question about her ability to attract and keep clients, but that was not the
46 controlling issue.
47

1	Q:	Did Simon Clark speak at the meeting regarding Ms. Polisi's partnership candidacy?
2		
3	A:	I really don't remember anything he had to say in particular other than the fact he was going
4		to abstain on the Polisi vote.
5		
6	Q:	Did he say anything about the work she did for him on the NCW case of the previous year?
7		
8	A:	Not that I recall. But his comments of the previous year were a matter of record.
9		
10	Q:	Did his abstention have any effect on the meeting?
11		
12	A:	No, not really. Because Simon was the chair, he would have only voted in the case of a tie
13		and the vote on Ms. Polisi, although it was close, was not a tie.
14		
15	Q:	Might any of your partners have made a negative inference from Clark's abstention?
16		
17	A:	They might have I suppose, but that didn't seem to be Clark's purpose. I think he was
18		embarrassed by the whole thing and abstained from voting in an attempt to rise above the
19		fray.
20		
21	Q:	Did he?
22		
23	A:	I suppose. Look, it was not his most shining hour. He should know better than to have sexual
24		relations with an associate, especially one that was working directly under him. He knows
25		it. The whole firm knows it. I hope this is the last time anything like this happens.

26

27 As expected, Cliff Fuller was Ms. Polisi's strongest advocate, but he too had to recognize
28 the potential for future problems if what we had seen was a pattern for Ms. Polisi. When we finally
29 voted not to nominate Ms. Polisi for partnership, Cliff tried to get us to agree to give her another
30 year. Most of us could not see how another good year would dispel our concerns about inconsistent
31 performance when faced with personal problems. It was this inconsistency, not Ms. Polisi's intellect
32 or talent, that was at issue. We then authorized her six months with the firm to find other
33 employment. The issue of non-equity partnership for Ms. Polisi was never reached because her
34 application was turned down on the basis of uneven work performance which would be unacceptable
35 for non-equity partners as well as equity partners.

36

37 I do not believe that Simon Clark used his substantial influence to harm Ms. Polisi's
38 partnership chances. I know for a fact that he did not talk to me. On balance, his comments at the
39 partnership nomination meeting were positive towards her, even though they were not glowing. The
40 fact of the break-up of the relationship between Ms. Polisi and Simon was never discussed openly
41 in the meeting, although I'm sure it was on the minds of all of us, to the extent that it shed light on
42 Ms. Polisi's ability to put personal considerations aside when working on her legal business. I
43 suppose it's possible that some of my partners might have thought that if they voted against Ms.
44 Polisi that they were doing Simon Clark a favor, but I doubt that happened. Simon could have easily
45 handled having Ms. Polisi as a partner if she was so nominated. If that was a problem and did cause
46 some of my partners to view her nomination negatively, I think that would be a legitimate business

1 decision. If a choice had to be made between Ms. Polisi and Simon Clark, and it did not happen here
2 in my opinion, the only correct business decision would be in favor of Simon Clark.
3
4   Simon did lose some influence in the firm after the dust had settled, and I know that he was
5 replaced in September of 2001, before the end of the normal five-year term, as chair of the litigation
6 section. The official statement was that he was stepping down because of his heavy litigation
7 schedule, but it would have been a good decision to get him out of a position of evaluating associates
8 if there was the potential of personal relationships between Simon and women associates developing.
9 This is especially so given the fact that Ms. Polisi filed a complaint against the law firm with the
10 EEOC in the summer of 2001. I know that we issued a general denial at the time and the next thing
11 we knew, the EEOC notified us that they had issued a "right to sue" letter to Ms. Polisi based on the
12 passage of 180 days. As a result this lawsuit is not a surprise.
13
14   One other fallout from this matter was that the firm lost Cliff Fuller as a partner. Apparently
15 Cliff and Simon had a falling out about some recommendation letters that Simon sent out concerning
16 Ms. Polisi, and this fact weighed heavily in favor, at least according to him, in Cliff accepting a
17 corporate position with NCW. His loss is a substantial one for the firm.
18
19   I understand that Ms. Polisi ended up taking a position on the law faculty at the University
20 of Nita. She certainly has the intellect for the job, and I'm sure she will succeed if she puts her mind
21 to it. A lot of the talent she displayed for litigation should transfer over well to teaching.
22
23

I have read this deposition and it is complete and accurate.

Jayne Post

Jayne Post

    Subscribed and sworn before me this 20th day of December, 2002.

Harry Gibbons

Harry Gibbons CSR
Certified Shorthand Reporter

    This deposition was given under oath at the offices of the plaintiff's counsel on November 29, 2002. This deposition was given under oath, read and signed by the deponent.

Assessment of Economic Loss

in the Matter of

Margaret Polisi v. Simon Clark and Parker & Gould

Prepared for Defense Counsel

by

Denise Williamson, Ph. D.

2003

This report was prepared for this file by Jerome Staller, Ph.D., and Stephanie Thomas, Ph.D., of the Center For Forensic Economic Studies, Suite 1200, 1608 Walnut Street, Philadelphia, PA 19103, (215) 546-5600.

Introduction

This report assesses the economic loss suffered by Margaret Polisi as a result of the alleged gender discrimination and defamation of character which occurred while she was án employee of the law firm, Parker & Gould. The economic loss consists of lost earnings. To prepare for this report we have reviewed all of the pleadings, depositions, and documents in this case, as well as those sources noted in this report.

Background

Ms. Polisi began her employment in 1986 with Parker & Gould (P & G) as a paralegal after receiving a bachelor's degree in political science from Nita University in 1984. In 1990, she entered Nita University School of Law at night. Ms. Polisi continued her work at P & G while attending law school, and after finishing her first year of school, she became a law clerk. The plaintiff graduated from law school in 1994, and was offered a position as an associate with P & G, which she accepted. In September of 1994, plaintiff began her career as a lawyer at P & G in the litigation section. During the course of her career, she had mixed reviews at P & G. In fact in 1999, plaintiff received a review grade of C, which served as a question mark as to her ability to achieve and maintain partner status. Plaintiff was reviewed for a possible partnership at P & G in June, 2001. At the time of her review, plaintiff had a mixed history of reviews at P & G, and also had brought no business to the firm. For these reasons, she was not accepted as a partner, and was given six months to secure alternative employment. Plaintiff left P & G in December of 2001.

Shortly after leaving P & G, plaintiff secured employment as first as an adjunct and then a tenure line professor at the University of Nita School of Law. While still a visiting professor, she received and rejected a lucrative offer from a major computer company, Nita Computer World (NCW), to join the office of corporate counsel. Plaintiff is currently forty-one years of age and employed as an Associate Professor of Law at the University of Nita School of Law.

Assumptions

The following assumptions were made in estimating the economic loss:

1) Expected Retirement

In our analysis, we have assumed that Plaintiff will retire at age 65.

2) Earnings Absent the Alleged Incidents

At the request of counsel, we have provided in our analysis two estimates of economic loss to plaintiff. Specifically, we have assessed plaintiff's alleged economic loss as the result of alleged gender discrimination and alleged defamation of character.

Discrimination Case

We have valued the potential economic loss to plaintiff as the result of alleged gender discrimination. Assuming that the plaintiff did suffer gender discrimination, then her potential earnings absent the discrimination are equal to her potential earnings as a partner at P & G.

According to recent articles in The American Lawyer, The Nita Inquirer, and the Nita Bar Journal, it is becoming increasingly more difficult for lawyers to attain partner status. Partnership offers have dropped off at many large law firms, and many firms including P & G are now offering non-equity partnerships in lieu of traditional equity partnerships historically offered to associates. At P & G, non-equity partnerships have been offered to two new partners in 2003 who had not attracted new clientele to the firm. All those associates who made partner in 2001 were offered traditional equity partnerships by P & G. Because plaintiff was denied a partnership, the issue of whether that partnership would have been an equity or non-equity partnership was never reached by the firm. Given that plaintiff had not, and was not likely to develop new business for P & G, we have assumed that she would have been offered, at best, a non-equity partnership and received the earnings outlined below:

Non-Equity Partner Earnings

Years	Salary
1	$130,000
3	$140,000
5	$160,000

This earnings profile was constructed from a national survey of lawyer earnings published in the Nita Bar Journal in 2002. We have valued these earnings from June of 2001, to the plaintiff's age 65.

Defamation Case

We have assumed that plaintiff did not suffer from gender discrimination, but that her character was allegedly defamed, thereby resulting in an economic loss due to an inability to market herself to other firms. Her inability to make partner at another law firm would be due to the same economic and personal factors limiting her ability at P & G. Any defamation would probably limit her to the associate level with another firm. These factors would include her own ability or inability to generate business for the firm, a lack of legal skills, a slow economy, etc.

According to the information from P & G, long-term associates are paid at the level of a sixth-year associate with inflationary increases given. Plaintiff had finished her sixth year at the time of her partnership decision. Her salary at the time was $122,721 per year. We have assumed that plaintiff would remain a long-term associate at P & G or at an alternative firm at a salary of $122,721 per year (2001 dollars). We have valued these earnings from June of 2001 to her age 65

3) Growth of Earnings

Past Growth

To estimate earnings growth in the past, we have relied upon the annual changes in the Compensation Per Hour Index (Economic Report of the President, February 2003; Economic Indicators, March 2003).

4) Discount Rate

Future earnings have been discounted to their present value. In doing so, we have assumed a long term nominal discount rate of 7.5%.

5) Earnings in Mitigation

Given the alleged gender discrimination and defamation, plaintiff has secured employment as a law school professor. In the spring of 2002, plaintiff taught her first law course as an adjunct professor at the University of Nita School of Law. She was then offered a full-time position for the 2002/2003 academic year as an associate professor in the law school. Plaintiff accepted the position with a starting salary of $75,000 per year.

In April of 2002, the plaintiff was offered a position in corporate counsel's office of NCW at a starting salary of $90,000. Plaintiff did not accept this position, but opted to stay at the law school at a lower salary. Given that a higher paying corporate counsel position was open to the plaintiff, she had the potential to earn higher wages; it was her own decision not to do so. As an aside, the existence of such an offer casts serious doubt as to the economic viability of the defamation claim.

In our analysis, we have provided two estimates of the plaintiff's earnings in mitigation. For the first estimate, we have assumed that the plaintiff would have mitigated her earnings, given the incident, by accepting the position with NCW at a starting salary of $90,000 per year (2002 dollars). Based upon information provided by Cliff Fuller at NCW, we have estimated the plaintiff's potential earnings as follows:

Potential Corporate Counsel Earnings at Nita Computer World

Years as Counsel	Salary
1	$120,000
3	$160,000
5	$225,000

As shown above, by the year, 2010, plaintiff's earnings as a corporate counselor are equal to those of a non-equity partner at P & G. Therefore, the earnings offset as of 2010, and there is no economic loss beyond that point.

It should be noted that earnings as a corporate counselor are greater than those as a long-term associate. Therefore, under the assumption that plaintiff would have remained a long-term associate absent the incident, and currently has the potential to be a corporate counselor, her economic loss would be zero.

In the second estimate, we have estimated the plaintiff's earnings in mitigation as her potential earnings as a law professor. According to her deposition testimony, in September of 2002, plaintiff's full-time associate professor's salary was $75,000 per year. We have assumed that plaintiff will remain in the teaching profession, and that by 2010 she will be promoted to a full professor position with a salary of $125,000 per year. This $125,000 figure is based on data provided by the American Association of Law Schools showing the average annual salaries for teachers in law schools.

It should be noted that we have valued earnings and benefits starting in June, 2001. For earnings from June 1 to December 31, 2001, we have used the plaintiff's salary as an associate at P & G, $122,721 per year.

Tables

Table 1 shows earnings as a non-equity partner at P & G to age 65.

Table 2 shows earnings as a long-term associate to age 65.

Table 3 shows earnings as a corporate counselor to age 65.

Table 4 shows earnings and fringe benefits as a law school professor to age 65.

Summary

As outlined in the Summary Table, the total economic loss to the plaintiff ranges from $0 to $305,696.

Summary Table

Margaret Polisi

DISCRIMINATION CASE

Earnings Absent the Incident $3,152,636

Less:

Earnings and Benefits Given the Incident

    (A) Corporate Counselor $5,468,851
    (B) Law School Professor $2,846,942

****
Total Economic Loss

    (A) Corporate Counselor $ 0
    (B) Law School Professor $ 305,696

DEFAMATION CASE

Earnings Absent the Incident $2,702,391

Less:

Earnings and Benefits Given the Incident

    (A) Corporate Counselor $5,468,851
    (B) Law School Professor $2,847,033

****
Total Economic Loss

    (A) Corporate Counselor $ 0
    (B) Law School Professor $ 0

EARNINGS ABSENT THE INCIDENT AS A NON-EQUITY PARTNER AT P & G

YEAR	AGE	EXPECTED EARNINGS
2001	39	65,000
2002	40	135,000
2003	41	140,000
PAST TOTAL		340,000
2004	42	146,163
2005	43	151,919
2006	44	148,032
2007	45	144,245
2008	46	140,555
2009	47	136,960
2010	48	133,456
2011	49	130,042
2012	50	126,716
2013	51	123,474
2014	52	120,315
2015	53	117,238
2016	54	114,238
2017	55	111,316
2018	56	108,468
2019	57	105,694
2020	58	102,990
2021	59	100,355
2022	60	97,788
2023	61	95,286
2024	62	92,849
2025	63	90,474
2026	64	88,159
2027	65	85,904
FUTURE TOTAL		2,812,636
TOTAL EARNINGS		3,152,636

EARNINGS ABSENT THE INCIDENT AS A LONG-TERM ASSOCIATE

YEAR	AGE	EXPECTED EARNINGS
2001	39	63,861
2002	40	128,550
2003	41	134,656
PAST TOTAL		327,067
2004	42	131,212
2005	43	127,855
2006	44	124,584
2007	45	121,397
2008	46	118,292
2009	47	115,266
2010	48	112,317
2011	49	109,444
2012	50	106,644
2013	51	103,916
2014	52	101,258
2015	53	98,667
2016	54	96,143
2017	55	93,684
2018	56	91,287
2019	57	88,952
2020	58	86,677
2021	59	84,459
2022	60	82,299
2023	61	80,193
2024	62	78,142
2025	63	76,143
2026	64	74,195
2027	65	72,297
FUTURE TOTAL		2,375,323
TOTAL EARNINGS		2,702,391

EARNINGS GIVEN THE INCIDENT AS A CORPORATE COUNSELOR

YEARS	AGES	EXPECTED EARNINGS	
2001 through 2003	39–41	323,861	(PAST TOTAL)
2004 through 2027	42–65	5,144,991	(FUTURE TOTAL)
TOTAL EARNINGS		5,468,852	

EARNINGS GIVEN THE INCIDENT AS A LAW SCHOOL PROFESSOR

YEARS	AGES	EXPECTED EARNINGS	
2001 through 2003	39–41	172,325	(PAST TOTAL)
2004 through 2027	42–65	2,674,708	(FUTURE TOTAL)
TOTAL		2,847,033	

To: Polisi File

From: Associate

Re: Denise Williamson, Ph.D. (Defendant's Expert)

Answers to interrogatories and independent investigation have revealed the following concerning defendant's expert, Dr. Williamson.

Dr. Williamson is forty-three years old and one of the founding members of Forensic Economics, Ltd. in Nita City. She started this business fifteen years ago, with a classmate from Nita University, John Pierce. Both she and Pierce received their Ph.D. degrees from Nita University in 1987, and after a year of postdoctoral work at the university, founded Forensic Economics, Ltd. They now employ ten economists and fifteen support staff, and their sole business is performing litigation support work for law firms.

Dr. Williamson testifies predominantly for defendants, and in recent years has developed a specialty in working for defense counsel in race, gender, and age discrimination cases. Several of her cases have involved claims for economic loss, due to discrimination, for members of the legal profession, so she has worked with the economics of the legal profession in the past.

Dr. Williamson's average fee for each case, including time spent testifying in deposition and trials, is between $9,000 and $10,000. Her time in preparing her report is billed at $350 per hour, and her fee for testifying at trial or deposition is $3,000 per day. Dr. Williamson has testified as an expert witness in excess of sixty times in the courts of Nita City (both state and federal). In all but three of those cases she testified as an expert witness for the defendant, in whose interest it was to minimize claimed economic losses.

Dr. Williamson has been retained by Parker & Gould as an expert witness for twenty-six cases in the past ten years. In all of those cases, P & G represented the defendant in a discrimination case. She has never worked with Simon Clark in any of those cases. This is the first matter where she has worked with defense counsel Emily Erway of the Speakman firm.

Dr. Williamson has no scholarly publications. She is a frequent speaker, however, in continuing legal education seminars sponsored by the Nita City and State Bar Associations on topics relating to forensic economics and effective methods for presenting such testimony.

Dr. Williamson responded to interrogatories that she recognized Dr. Gerald Morris' book, *Forensic Economics*, (5th ed. Nita University Press, 2002) as a generally authoritative source in the area of forensic economics, but did not rely on the text specifically in reaching her opinion in this case. Dr. Morris was a professor at Nita University while Dr. Williamson was both an undergraduate and graduate student. She took a number of courses from him and did well academically, but did not have a close professional relationship, i.e. he did not advise her on her thesis or act as a reference for her.

REPORT OF ECONOMIC LOSS

POLISI v. CLARK AND PARKER & GOULD

PREPARED FOR COUNSEL FOR THE PLAINTIFF

BY GERALD MORRIS, PH.D.

2003

This report was prepared for this file by Jerome Staller, Ph.D., and Stephanie Thomas, Ph.D., of The Center For Forensic Economic Studies, Suite 1200, 1608 Walnut Street, Philadelphia, PA 19103, (215) 546-5600.

Report of Economic Loss

Polisi v. Clark and Parker & Gould

2003

INTRODUCTION

This report assesses the economic loss suffered by Margaret Polisi as a result of the alleged gender discrimination and defamation of character, which occurred while she was an employee of the Defendant law firm, Parker & Gould (P & G), and under the supervision of Defendant Clark. The economic loss consists of lost earnings. In reaching these conclusions we have relied on all of the pleadings and other discovery in this case, as well as those other sources that are specifically mentioned in this report.

BACKGROUND

After receiving a bachelor's degree in political science from Nita University in 1984, Ms. Polisi began her employment in 1986 as a paralegal at P & G. In 1990 she entered a four-year law degree program in the evening division at the University of Nita School of Law. Ms. Polisi continued to work for the Defendant law firm as a law clerk during her period of attendance at the law school, and during this time received very good performance reviews from her supervisors. Ms. Polisi graduated first in her class from law school in 1994 and was offered and accepted a position as an associate with P & G. She was assigned to the litigation section of the firm and worked in that section from September of 1994 through December of 2001. In June of 2001, Ms. Polisi was considered for a partnership with the firm, but despite excellent work reviews by her supervisors, was not accepted. She was terminated by the firm, effective December 31, 2001.

After undergoing a period of psychological trauma brought on by a hostile work environment, she was able to accept a part-time teaching position at the University of Nita School of Law. Eventually she was offered a tenure-line appointment to the law school which commenced in September of 2002. Ms. Polisi in currently 41 years old and employed as an Associate Professor of Law at the University of Nita.

ASSUMPTIONS

The following assumptions were made in estimating the economic loss to Ms. Polisi:

1. Retirement Age

In our analysis we have assumed that Ms. Polisi will work until the age of 65.

2. Potential Earnings Absent Discrimination and Defamation

At counsel's request, we have provided in our analysis two estimates of the economic loss to Ms. Polisi. We have assessed Ms. Polisi's alleged economic loss as a result of (a) gender discrimination and (b) defamation of character.

Discrimination

We have assumed that the economic loss to Ms. Polisi is a direct result of the alleged gender discrimination she incurred as an employee at P & G. We have valued her potential earnings absent the discrimination as Ms. Polisi's potential earnings as a partner at P & G. According to the information received from P & G, their partners have the following earning pattern:

Partner Earnings at Parker & Gould

Years as Partner	Number of Partners	Median	Mean	Range
1	4	130,000	127,500	110,000 to 140,000
3	6	160,000	155,000	120,000 to 200,000
5	3	280,000	260,000	200,000 to 300,000
7	4	350,000	356,250	225,000 to 500,000
10	5	460,000	475,000	275,000 to 600,000
20	4	475,000	500,000	300,000 to 750,000

We have assumed that Ms. Polisi would have become a partner at P & G in June, 2001, and would have had earnings following the pattern outlined above for mean earnings. We have valued earnings from June of 2001 to Ms. Polisi's age 65.

Defamation

We have assumed that Ms. Polisi did not suffer from gender discrimination, but that her character was defamed thereby resulting in an economic loss. Absent the defamation, Ms. Polisi may have secured alternative employment at another law firm. However, given the alleged defamation, she was unable to secure alternative employment at another law firm. Her potential earnings absent the defamation are equal to earnings at an alternative law firm. We have assumed that she would have secured such employment as of January 1, 2002. We have further assumed that she would have remained an associate until January 1, 2005 at the alternative firm and then would have been promoted to partner. Our assumption is that her earnings would have followed the pattern set out below:

Year	Position	Median Earnings (2003 dollars)
2002	Associate	$ 90,000
2003	Associate	100,000
2004	Associate	110,000
2005	Partner	150,000
2007	Partner	175,000
2009	Partner	200,000
2011	Partner	225,000
2014	Partner	250,000
2024	Partner	300,000

This earnings pattern has been derived reviewing a national survey of lawyer earning published in the Nita Bar Journal in 2002. In this estimate we have assumed that Ms. Polisi's earnings would have been equal to the median earnings for all partners. This is in contrast to potential earnings at P & G, a top level law firm with the earnings to match.

3. Future Growth of Earnings

Earnings growth after 2002 was estimated to be 6.61% per year. This rate represents the average annual rate of change in the Compensation Per Hour Index from 1982 to 2002 (Economic Report of the President, February 2003; Economic Indicators, March, 2003.

4. Discount Rate

We have discounted future earnings to their present value. Based on a review of information in this matter and currently prevailing interest rates, we have used a nominal rate of 5%.

5. Earnings in Mitigation

In the spring of 2002, Ms. Polisi became and adjunct professor at the University of Nita School of Law. She became a member of the tenure-line faculty in September of 2002. Her starting salary was $75,000 per year.

We have assumed that Ms. Polisi will remain in the teaching profession and that by 2010 she will be promoted to a full professor position with a salary of $95,000 per year. This figure is based upon data from the University of Nita School of Law as to the average annual salaries of full professors.

It should be noted that we have valued earnings starting in June of 2001. For earnings from June 1 to December 31, 2001 we have used Ms. Polisi's salary as an associate at P & G, $122,721.

6. Future Growth and Discounting of Earnings

We have utilized the same future growth and discounting methodologies as described earlier.

TABLES

Table 1 shows earnings as a partner at P & G to age 65.

Table 2 shows earnings as an associate/partner at an alternative law firm to age 65.

Table 3 shows earnings as a law professor to age 65.

SUMMARY

As outlined in the Summary Table, the total economic loss to Ms. Polisi ranges from $4,596,832 to $10,838,333.

SUMMARY TABLE

MARGARET POLISI

DISCRIMINATION

Earnings Absent the Incident	$13,688,341
Less:	
Earnings Given the Incident	$2,850,009
Total Economic Loss	$10,838,332

DEFAMATION

Earnings Absent the Incident	$7,446,840
Less:	
Earnings Given the Incident	$2,850,009
Total Economic Loss	$4,596,831

TABLE I

EARNINGS ABSENT THE INCIDENT AS A PARTNER AT P & G

PAST TOTAL EARNINGS (2001 - 2003)	$ 359,861
FUTURE TOTAL EARNINGS (2004 - 2027)	$13,328,480
TOTAL EARNINGS	$13,688,341

TABLE 2

EARNINGS ABSENT THE INCIDENT AS AN ASSOCIATE/ PARTNER

AT ANOTHER FIRM

PAST TOTAL EARNINGS (2002 - 2003)	$ 253,861
FUTURE TOTAL EARNINGS (2004 - 2027)	$7,192,979
TOTAL EARNINGS	$7,446,840

TABLE 3

EARNINGS GIVEN THE INCIDENT AS A LAW SCHOOL PROFESSOR

PAST TOTAL EARNINGS (2001-2 - 2003)	$ 172,235
FUTURE TOTAL EARNINGS (2004 - 2027)	$2,677,774
TOTAL EARNINGS	$2,850,009

To: Polisi File

From: Associate

Re: Gerald Morris, Ph.D. (Plaintiff's Expert)

The following information has been obtained from answers to interrogatories and an independent investigation into the background of Dr. Morris.

Dr. Morris is fifty-two years old and the chair of the Department of Economics at Nita University. He obtained his Ph.D. in economics in 1978 from the University of Pennsylvania, and has been employed as a professor at Nita University since then. Dr. Morris received tenure in 1983, a year earlier than normal, and was promoted to full professor three years later. In 1993 he was named the Charles Burkett Professor of Economics, the most important chair in the Economics Department at Nita University. He has been the chair of the Economics Department for the past eight years.

Dr. Morris has written over 100 books and articles in his career. He is the author of a book entitled, *Forensic Economics*, which is generally regarded as a leading text in the field. It is used at over 100 universities around the world as the standard text on the topic of forensic economics. The book was originally published in 1988 by Nita University Press, and is currently in its fifth edition.

Dr. Morris does not testify regularly as an expert witness. His last appearance as an expert was eight years ago when he appeared on behalf of a colleague in the university who was seriously injured in an automobile accident. His professional life is geared toward the academic study of economics, and he does not have an active consulting business that would cause him to serve as an expert witness with any regularity. He claims no particular expertise in the economics of the legal profession, but views it as a part of the service sector of the economy.

Dr. Morris does not know Ms. Polisi personally, except for his interaction with her in this case, but agreed to testify on her behalf after a request was made by his good friend, Dean Martin Purcell of the Nita University School of Law, where Ms. Polisi is employed as an Associate Professor of Law.

Dr. Morris was an instructor at Nita University while Dr. Williamson (the defendant's expert) was both an undergraduate and graduate student. He recalls that she was a good student, but not an outstanding one.

I have learned that Dr. Morris was recently turned down for a large grant made by the Parker Foundation, which is named for one of the founding partners of Parker & Gould. The foundation is managed by the Parker & Gould law firm. The grant which was made instead to Dr. Harriet Graham of Nita State University was in the amount of $750,000 for a three-year study on predicting wage growth patterns in service industries for the next twenty years. Dr. Morris and Dr. Graham were the finalists for the grant.

TABLE OF EXHIBITS

EXHIBIT NUMBER	CONTENT
1	Polisi Resume
2	Hiring Letter - P & G to Polisi
3 A–G	Polisi Evaluation Forms
4 A–F	Polisi Salary Letters
5 A–H	DeAngelo Evaluation Forms
6	NCW Commendation Letter Re: Polisi
7 A & B	P & G 1994 Associates, Class Grades, and Billable Hours Records
8	7/ 9/-2 Phone Log for Simon Clark
9	7/15/-2 Phone Log for Simon Clark
10	Fuller Draft of Clark Recommendation Letter for Polisi
11	Clark Letter to Randall Re: Polisi
12	Clark Letter to Miller Re: Polisi
13	Clark Letter to Warren Re: Polisi
14	EEOC Notice of Charge of Discrimination
15	P & G Response to Exhibit 14
16	EEOC Right to Sue Letter
17	Clark Letter to Purcell Re: Polisi
18	Affidavit of John Randall

EXHIBIT 1

RESUME

MARGARET M. POLISI

EDUCATION:

University of Nita, B.A. Political Science, 1984
Honors: Phi Beta Kappa

University of Nita School of Law, J.D., 1994
Honors: Magna Cum Laude; Mary & William Walsh Award
For Legal Scholarship (Graduated First in Class); Thomas Knox
Award for Excellence in Law Review Editing.
Activities: Nita University Law Review, 1991 – 1994, Articles
Editor, Volume 82.

EMPLOYMENT:

University of Nita School of Law, Nita City
Associate Professor of Law, Since 2002

Parker & Gould, Four Independence Square, Nita City
Associate – 1994 – 2001 – Worked on the full range civil litigation
matters. Duties included research, pretrial and trial writing, taking
and defending depositions, arguing motions, and examination of
witnesses.
Litigation Law Clerk – 1991 – 1994
Litigation Paralegal – 1986 – 1991

PUBLICATIONS:

WORK PRODUCT AND THE RIGHT TO REFRESHING DOCU-
MENTS: SOMETHING'S GOT TO GIVE, 89 U. Nita L. Rev 45,
(2001).

LAWYER CONFLICTS OF INTEREST IN MULTI-PARTY
ANTITRUST LITIGATION, 58 Conwell U. L. Rev, 2002.

COURSES TAUGHT: Civil Procedure, Evidence, Seminar on Complex Civil Litigation

PERSONAL:

Address: 7010 Greenhill Road
          Nita City, Nita

Phone: 555-8949 (Work)
          555-2892 (Home)

Two Children: David and Maureen

Excellent Health. Enjoy tennis, hiking, water sports, and travel.

EXHIBIT 2

— PARKER & GOULD —
Four Independence Square
Nita City, Nita

July 1, 1994

Ms. Margaret Polisi
Parker & Gould
Four Independence Square
Nita City, Nita

Dear Ms. Polisi,

This is to confirm that you have accepted a position with the law firm of Parker & Gould as an associate in our litigation department. Your beginning annual salary will be $85,000.00.

You will be required to assume the normal responsibilities of an associate with the firm, and it is understood that your position with the firm will be evaluated each year.

As you are currently employed as a law clerk, you are familiar with the benefits package at P & G, so I will not cover them specifically in this letter. If you have any questions concerning our benefits package, please contact Mary Williamson in our benefits office. As you know, you will receive one month's salary to compensate you for your time spent in studying for the bar examination.

Please notify me at your earliest convenience as to your anticipated starting date with the firm. We look forward to your coming on board.

If the above terms and conditions are acceptable to you, please indicate same by signing and returning one copy of this letter.

Welcome.

Sincerely,

Charles Milton, Chair
Litigation Section

Signed: _Margaret Polisi_
Margaret Polisi

Date: 7-10-1994

—— *PARKER & GOULD* ——
Four Independence Square
Nita City, Nita

MEMORANDUM

TO: M. Polisi File

FROM: C. Milton, Chair Litigation Section   *CM*

RE: First-Year Evaluation

DATE: September 10, 1995

****

GRADE: C

HOURS: 1770

NARRATIVE: Ms. Polisi had an acceptable first year. Writing needs improvement. Hours are acceptable for a first-year associate but we expect improvement here also. Bright, articulate. Two associates in class with a B, seven others with a C. 3% raise.

—— *PARKER & GOULD* ——
Four Independence Square
Nita City, Nita

MEMORANDUM

TO: M. Polisi File

FROM: C. Milton, Chair Litigation Section *CM*

RE: Second-Year Evaluation

DATE: September 13, 1996

****

GRADE: B

HOURS: 1960

NARRATIVE: Ms. Polisi had a good second year. Improvement noted in both writing style and in billable hours. Remains some small question concerning analytical ability. Some questions raised concerning aggressiveness. Three other associates in class with a B. 5% raise.

—— *PARKER & GOULD* ——
Four Independence Square
Nita City, Nita

MEMORANDUM

TO: M. Polisi File

FROM: C. Milton, Chair Litigation Section *CM*

RE: Third-Year Evaluation

DATE: September 11, 1997

****

GRADE: B

HOURS: 2020

NARRATIVE: Ms. Polisi had a good third year. Research and writing skills are acceptable. Hours acceptable. Positive comments on analytical skill with one exception. Still some questions concerning aggressiveness. Three other associates in class with a B. 5% raise.

—— *PARKER & GOULD* ——
Four Independence Square
Nita City, Nita

MEMORANDUM

TO: M. Polisi File

FROM: C. Milton, Chair Litigation Section   *CM*

RE: Fourth-Year Evaluation

DATE: September 13, 1998

****

GRADE: B

HOURS: 2040

NARRATIVE: Ms. Polisi had a good year at the firm. Research, analysis and writing skills remain strong. Still some question concerning toughness and lack of aggressiveness. Question raised concerning failure to travel outside of Nita area for extended periods. Hours acceptable. Four other associates in class with a B. 5% raise. $10,000.00 market adjustment.

—— *PARKER & GOULD* ——
Four Independence Square
Nita City, Nita

MEMORANDUM

TO: M. Polisi File

FROM: S. Clark, Chair Litigation Section *SC*

RE: Fifth-Year Evaluation

DATE: September 14, 1999

****

GRADE: C

HOURS: 1830

NARRATIVE: Ms. Polisi had a mediocre year at the firm. Her bill-
             able hours are not acceptable. Also received some
             negative comments on quality of analytical ability.
             Given option of leaving firm with good recommendation,
             attempted placement with client or attempt to improve
             substantially. Chooses to remain with firm. One associ-
             ate in class with an A. Two associates in class with a
             B. Six other associates in class with a C. 3% raise.

—— *PARKER & GOULD* ——
Four Independence Square
Nita City, Nita

MEMORANDUM

TO: M. Polisi File

FROM: S. Clark, Chair Litigation Section   *SC*

RE: Sixth-Year Evaluation

DATE: September 14, 2000

****

GRADE: A

HOURS: 2300

NARRATIVE: Ms. Polisi had an excellent year. Billable hours are very good. NCW complimentary on her work in recent case. Good candidate for partnership. One other associate in class with an A. 7% raise.

—— *PARKER & GOULD* ——
Four Independence Square
Nita City, Nita

MEMORANDUM

TO: M. Polisi

FROM: C. Fuller, Deputy Chair, Litigation Section *C. F.*

RE: Partnership Evaluation - Seventh Year

DATE: June 2, 2001

****

GRADE: B

HOURS: 1445 (As of June 1, 2001)

NARRATIVE: Ms. Polisi had a good fall, and a mediocre winter and spring. Billable hours were fine (895) for September 2000. January 2001 drop-off to 550 hours for February 2001 through May 2001, which are not acceptable for that period. Some questions raised concerning quality of written product and toughness. Advised to put partnership decision over until 2002. Ms. Polisi declines advice. Two associates in partnership class with an A. One other associate in partnership class with a B.

June 15, 2001 - Partnership nomination by Litigation Section declined. Given until December 15, 2001, to find another position.

—— PARKER & GOULD ——
Four Independence Square
Nita City, Nita

September 20, 1995

Ms. Margaret Polisi
Parker & Gould
Four Independence Square
Nita City, Nita

Dear Ms. Polisi,

This is to confirm that your salary for the year September 1995 through September 1996 will be $87,550.00. This represents a merit raise of 3%.

Your contributions to the firm are appreciated.

Sincerely,

Charles Milton, Chair
Litigation Section

—— *PARKER & GOULD* ——
Four Independence Square
Nita City, Nita

September 22, 1996

Ms. Margaret Polisi
Parker & Gould
Four Independence Square
Nita City, Nita

Dear Ms. Polisi,

This is to confirm that your salary for the year September 1996 through September 1997 will be $91,928.00. This represents a merit raise of 5%.

Your contributions to the firm are appreciated.

Sincerely,

Charles Milton, Chair
Litigation Section

—— PARKER & GOULD ——
Four Independence Square
Nita City, Nita

September 18, 1997

Ms. Margaret Polisi
Parker & Gould
Four Independence Square
Nita City, Nita

Dear Ms. Polisi,

This is to confirm that your salary for the year September 1997 through September 1998 will be $96,525.00. This represents a merit raise of 5%.

Your contributions to the firm are appreciated.

Sincerely,

Charles Milton, Chair
Litigation Section

——— PARKER & GOULD ———
Four Independence Square
Nita City, Nita

September 21, 1998

Ms. Margaret Polisi
Parker & Gould
Four Independence Square
Nita City, Nita

Dear Ms. Polisi,

This is to confirm that your salary for the year September 1998
through September 1999 will be $111,352.00. This represents a
merit raise of 5% and a market adjustment of $10,000.00.

Your contributions to the firm are appreciated.

Sincerely,

Charles Milton, Chair
Litigation Section

—— *PARKER & GOULD* ——
Four Independence Square
Nita City, Nita

September 22, 1999

Ms. Margaret Polisi
Parker & Gould
Four Independence Square
Nita City, Nita

Dear Ms. Polisi,

This is to confirm that your salary for the year September 1999 through September 2000 will be $114,693.00. This represents a merit raise of 3%.

The firm values your contributions and we look forward to a productive year.

Sincerely yours,

Simon Clark

Simon Clark, Chair
Litigation Section

—— *PARKER & GOULD* ——
Four Independence Square
Nita City, Nita

September 24, 2000

Ms. Margaret Polisi
Parker & Gould
Four Independence Square
Nita City, Nita

Dear Ms. Polisi,

This is to confirm that your salary for the year September 2000 through September 2001 will be $122,721. This represents a merit raise of 7%.

The firms values your contributions and we look forward to a productive year.

Warm regards,

Simon Clark, Chair
Litigation Section

—— *PARKER & GOULD* ——
Four Independence Square
Nita City, Nita

MEMORANDUM

TO: M. DeAngelo File

FROM: C. Milton, Chair Litigation Section *CM*

RE: First-Year Evaluation

DATE: September 9, 1995

****

GRADE: B

HOURS: 1880

NARRATIVE: Mr. DeAngelo had a good first year. Hours are good
            for a first year. Writing style needs work.
            Analytical skills acceptable. Good aggressiveness
            in seeking out assignments. One other associate in
            class with a B. 5% raise.

—— *PARKER & GOULD* ——
Four Independence Square
Nita City, Nita

MEMORANDUM

TO: M. DeAngelo File

FROM: C. Milton, Chair Litigation Section *CM*

RE: Second-Year Evaluation

DATE: September 11, 1996

****

GRADE: B

HOURS: 1910

NARRATIVE: Mr. DeAngelo had a good second year. His billable
           hours are acceptable. Writing style improving.
           Analysis acceptable. Good aggressiveness and
           mental toughness. Three other associates in class
           with a B. 5% raise.

—— *PARKER & GOULD* ——
Four Independence Square
Nita City, Nita

MEMORANDUM

TO: M. DeAngelo File

FROM: C. Milton, Chair Litigation Section *CM*

RE: Third-Year Evaluation

DATE: September 12, 1997

****

GRADE: B

HOURS: 2100

NARRATIVE: Mr. DeAngelo had a good year. Hours at top of class. Writing style improved. Acceptable analytical ability. Very tough and resilient. Three other associates in class with a B. 5% raise.

—— PARKER & GOULD ——
Four Independence Square
Nita City, Nita

MEMORANDUM

TO: M. DeAngelo File

FROM: C. Milton, Chair Litigation Section *CM*

RE: Fourth-Year Evaluation

DATE: September 10, 1998

****

GRADE: B

HOURS: 2220

NARRATIVE: Mr. DeAngelo had a good year. Billable hours at top of his class. Uniform good skills. Some question about how he will do in client relations. Good aggressiveness. Four other associates in class with a B. 5% raise. $10,000.00 market adjustment.

—— *PARKER & GOULD* ——
Four Independence Square
Nita City, Nita

MEMORANDUM

TO: M. DeAngelo File

FROM: S. Clark, Chair Litigation Section *SC*

RE: Fifth-Year Evaluation

DATE: September 13, 1999

****

GRADE: B

HOURS: 2260

NARRATIVE: Another solid year for Mr. DeAngelo. Hours at the
           top of class. Good candidate for partnership, but
           looking for spark. Some questions concerning
           client relations. Skills uniformly good. One
           associate in class with an A. One other associate
           in class with a B. 5% raise.

—— *PARKER & GOULD* ——
Four Independence Square
Nita City, Nita

MEMORANDUM

TO: M. DeAngelo File

FROM: S. Clark, Chair Litigation Section *SC*

RE: Sixth-Year Evaluation

DATE: September 13, 2000

****

GRADE: B

HOURS: 2210

NARRATIVE: Mr. DeAngelo has another solid year at the firm.
           Billable hours are among firm's highest for
           associates. Skills uniformly good but not stellar
           in any particular area. Continuing question
           concerning client relations. Good partnership
           potential. Two associates in class with an A. One
           other associate in class with B. 5% raise.

—— *PARKER & GOULD* ——
Four Independence Square
Nita City, Nita

MEMORANDUM

TO: M. DeAngelo File

FROM: S. Clark, Chair Litigation Section *SC*

RE: Partnership Evaluation - Seventh Year

DATE: June 2, 2001

****

GRADE: B

HOURS: 1700 (As of June 1, 2001)

NARRATIVE: Mr. DeAngelo is a solid performer. Has regained status as top billing associate. Solid in all respects. Only questions are concerning client relations and ability to attract and/or keep clients. Two associates in partnership class with an A. One other associate with a B.

June 15, 2001 - On recommendation of litigation partnership, decision put over to June, 2002. 5% raise effective June 1, 2001.

—— *PARKER & GOULD* ——
Four Independence Square
Nita City, Nita

MEMORANDUM

TO: M. DeAngelo File

FROM: R. Bryant, Chair Litigation Section   *RB*

RE: Partnership Evaluation - Eighth Year

DATE: June 2, 2002

****

GRADE: A

HOURS: 2380

NARRATIVE: Mr. DeAngelo had an excellent year. Skills are
           uniformly good. Billable hours are highest for all
           associates. Performed very well in complex trial
           in examination of experts. Attracted new client to
           the firm. One other associate in partnership class
           with an A.

           June 16, 2002 - Partnership nomination made by
           litigation section.

EXHIBIT 6

NITA COMPUTER WORLD
"A WORLD BETTER"
1550 SCIENCE DRIVE
NITA CITY, NITA

July 8, 2000

Mr. Simon Clark
Parker & Gould
Four Independence Square
Nita City, Nita

Dear Simon:

I have just returned from a Board of Directors Meeting for the company and wanted to report how pleased the Board is over the outcome in our most recent litigation handled by you and your firm. As you may know, several of the companies who failed to settle the case were hit pretty hard by the jury in that case and the work of you and your team, together with your wise counsel, saved us a great deal of money.

Please pass on my thanks to your litigation team. In particular, I should tell you that I was most impressed with the performance, as I observed it, of your associate, Maggie Polisi. She did a fine job in arguing for our trade secret protective order, the positive result of which positioned us well for settlement of the case. I do not know her status at the firm, but NCW would be pleased to have her work on other matters for us in the future. Specifically, we have been sued in a matter that is being handled by Cliff Fuller in which a similar issue of trade secrets is involved, and I hope that she can be assigned to that case.

I trust that you and your team enjoyed your recent trip. I'll get a full report when we meet next week.

Warm regards,

Howard Meltzer
Vice President
General Counsel

cc: Ms. Margaret Polisi
    Parker & Gould

—— PARKER & GOULD ——
Four Independence Square
Nita City, Nita

COMPILATION OF EMPLOYMENT RECORDS FOR ASSOCIATES ENTERING 1994 WHILE ON PARTNERSHIP TRACK

ENTRIES SHOW NAME OF ASSOCIATE, GRADE & BILLABLE HOURS FOR EACH YEAR WITH FIRM

NAME	1995	1996	1997	1998	1999	2000	2001
DeAngelo, Michael	B 1880	B 1910	B 2100	B 2220	B 2260	B 2210	B 2250
Eisenberg, David	D 1740	D 1800					
Forsano, Elizabeth	C 1700	C 1820	C 1860	C 1900			
Hancock, Mark	C 1750	C 1850	B 2060	B 2160	B 2210	B 2190	A 1650*
Jenner, Jennifer	D 1650	C 1820					
Kramer, Roger	B 1850	B 1900	B 1910	B 1940	A 2070	A 2050	A 1590*
Levy, Esther	C 1790	C 1840	C 1890				
Lucas, Ralph	D 1740	C 1800	C 1810	C 1890	C 1940		
Marin, John	D 1710	D 1740					
Medovsky, Gregory	D 1740	C 1810	C 1860	C 1910	C 1960		
Nathans, Howard	C 1760	C 1800	D 1780				
Opperheim, Richard	D 1650	C 1850	C 1950	P/A**			
Polisi, Margaret	C 1770	B 1960	B 2020	B 2040	C 1830	A 2300	B 1750

COMPILATION OF EMPLOYMENT RECORDS - ASSOCIATES ENTERING 1994
    (CONTINUE)

NAME	1995	1996	1997	1998	1999	2000	2001
Polen, Craig	C 1780	C 1880					
Richards, Harriet	C 1780	C 1840	C 1880	C 1980			
Sherman, Gary	B 1850	B 1920	C 1880	B 2010			
Tomlinson, Mary	C 1800	C 1820	C 1890	P/A**			
Washburn, Peter	C 1740	C 1880	D 1650				
Wasilewski, Kathryn	C 1780	C 1860	C 1900	C 1930	C 1960		

* Elected to partnership, June, 2001. Hours reflect those accumulated through June 1, 2001.

**Accepted position as permanent associate with firm. No longer on partnership track.

EXHIBIT 8

——PARKER & GOULD——
Four Independence Square
Nita City, Nita

INCOMING PHONE LOG

NAME: S. Clark   **SECRETARY:** Cary Jones

DATE	PERSON CALLING	PHONE NUMBER	MESSAGE
7/9/01	David Greenburg IRS	202-544-1770	Please call re: Tax Audit ✓
7/9/01	Bill Grayson NCW	530-1000	Please call re: Cal. litigation ✓
7/9/01	Mary Carson Nita Country Club	555-1444 member/guest	Please call re: tournament ✓
7/9/01	John Randall Morrison & Farrow	555-5880 Polisi	Please call re: recommendation ✓
7/9/01	Amanda	Home or car	Dinner with Mitchells ✓
7/9/01	Gerry Mason Cooper & Davis	215-878-3000	Please call re: Rogers v. Preston Tools ✓

EXHIBIT 9

—— *PARKER & GOULD* ——
Four Independence Square
Nita City, Nita

INCOMING PHONE LOG

NAME: Simon Clark   **SECRETARY:** Cary Jones

DATE	PERSON CALLING	PHONE NUMBER	MESSAGE
7/15/01	Bill Grayson NCW	530-1000	Call re: Cal. litigation ✓
7/15/01	Harriet Miller Carter & Carroll	441-4100	Please call re: Polisi recommendation ✓
7/15/01	Rob Bryant	x8110	Please call ✓
7/15/01	Amanda	At Club	Dinner with Meltons ✓
7/15/01	Roger Warren Melinson & Capps	487-6000	Please call re: Polisi recommendation ✓
7/15/01	Andy Freeman Cooper & Davis	215-878-3000	Please call re: Rogers v. Preston Tools ✓ outstanding interrogatories

EXHIBIT 10

—— *PARKER & GOULD* ——
Four Independence Square
Nita City, Nita

Dear   ,

It is with great pleasure that I write you concerning Ms. Margaret Polisi who has applied for a position with your firm. Over the past several years I have worked closely with her and feel well qualified to evaluate her abilities as a litigator.

Ms. Polisi came to us after a distinguished career at the University of Nita School of Law where she was an Editor of the Law Review and graduated first in her class. During her time at Parker & Gould she has worked on the most sophisticated of matters and has demonstrated enormous talent as a litigator.

She possesses analytical prowess, a talent for precision and persuasiveness in writing, and the ability to articulate her clients' positions in effective oral advocacy. She has, quite frankly, excelled in all areas of lawyering.

In addition to her superb skills, Ms. Polisi has shown excellent maturity and does very well in client interaction. In fact, in a recent case, involving one of our most sophisticated clients, she was commended by the client, in writing, at the successful conclusion of the case.

In closing, let me say that you will have a difficult time finding a better addition to your firm than Ms. Polisi. If I can be of further assistance, please do not hesitate to call.

Sincerely,

Simon Clark

Simon —
This is the
recommendation
letter. C. F.

EXHIBIT 11

—— PARKER & GOULD ——
Four Independence Square
Nita City, Nita

June 27, 2001

Mr. John Randall
Morrison & Farrow
Four Courthouse Square
Nita City, Nita

Dear John,

It is with great pleasure that I write in recommendation of
Ms. Margaret Polisi for a position with your firm. Although my
opportunities to work with her have been limited because of
some travel restrictions she imposed, I have worked with her
on several cases which provide me with an adequate basis to
evaluate her abilities.

Ms. Polisi possesses a fine mind and generally applies it to
her work. She has performed the full range of associate duties
at the firm and her work has been well received by myself and
my partners. Her analytical skills are solid, and she presents
her analysis in a clear writing style. In addition, while her
opportunities have been limited, she has taken and defended
depositions and represented our clients in motion practice
before various courts.

In closing, let me say that a decision to hire Ms. Polisi for
an associate's position with your firm would be a good one.
I am sure that you will be satisfied with her performance. If
I can be of further assistance, please feel free to call.

Warm regards,

Simon Clark

Simon Clark, Chair
Litigation Section

*No further interview
not interested.*

JR

*P.S. John -- be careful
on this one. Call me.
SC*

EXHIBIT 12

—— *PARKER & GOULD* ——
Four Independence Square
Nita City, Nita

July 7, 2001

Ms. Harriet Miller
Carter & Carroll
410 Pine Street
Nita City, Nita

Dear Ms. Miller,

It is with great pleasure that I write in recommendation of Ms. Margaret Polisi for a position with your firm. Although my opportunities to work with her have been limited because of some travel restrictions she imposed, I have worked with her on several cases which provide me with an adequate basis to evaluate her abilities.

Ms. Polisi possesses a fine mind and generally applies it to her work. She has performed the full range of associate duties at the firm and her work has been well received by myself and my partners. Her analytical skills are solid, and she presents her analysis in a clear writing style. In addition, while her opportunities have been limited, she has taken and defended depositions and represented our clients in motion practice before various courts.

In closing, let me say that a decision to hire Ms. Polisi for an associate's position with your firm would be a good one. I am sure that you will be satisfied with her performance. If I can be of further assistance, please feel free to call.

Sincerely yours,

Simon Clark

Simon Clark, Chair
Litigation Section

EXHIBIT 13

—— *PARKER & GOULD* ——
Four Independence Square
Nita City, Nita

July 8, 2001

Mr. Roger Warren
Melinson & Capps
1420 JFK Boulevard
Nita City, Nita

Dear Roger,

It is with great pleasure that I write in recommendation of
Ms. Margaret Polisi for a position with your firm. Although my
opportunities to work with her have been limited because of
some travel restrictions she imposed, I have worked with her
on several cases which provide me with an adequate basis to
evaluate her abilities.

Ms. Polisi possesses a fine mind and generally applied it to
her work. She has performed the full range of associate duties
at the firm and her work has been well received by myself and
my partners. Her analytical skills are solid, and she presents
her analysis in a clear writing style. In addition, while her
opportunities have been limited, she has taken and defended
depositions and represented our clients in motion practice in
various courts.

In closing, let me say that a decision to hire Ms. Polisi for
an associate's position with your firm would be a good one.
I am sure that you will be satisfied with her performance. If
I can be of further assistance, please feel free to call.

Warm regards,

Simon Clark

Simon Clark, Chair
Litigation Section

Spoke to S.C
- Not a good
lateral candidate.
R.W.

EXHIBIT 14

EQUAL EMPLOYMENT OPPORTUNITY COMMISSION	PERSON FILING CHARGE Margaret Polisi

THIS PERSON (check one)

[X] CLAIMS TO BE AGGRIEVED

[ ] IS FILING ON BEHALF OF ANOTHER

DATE OF ALLEGED VIOLATION
Earliest
1/1/01

PLACE OF ALLEGED VIOLATION
Nita City, Nita

CHARGE NUMBER
2001-49985

Parker & Gould
Four Independence Square
Nita City, Nita

NOTICE OF CHARGE OF DISCRIMINATION
(See EEOC "Rules and Regulations" before completing this Form)

You are hereby notified that a charge of employment discrimination has been filed against your organization under:

[X] TITLE VII OF THE CIVIL RIGHTS ACT OF 1964

[ ] THE AGE DISCRIMINATION IN EMPLOYMENT ACT OF 1967

[ ] THE AMERICANS WITH DISABILITIES ACT

[ ] THE EQUAL PAY ACT (29 U.S.C, SECT. 206(d)) investigation will be conducted concurrently with our investigation of this charge.

The boxes checked below apply to your organization:

1. [ ] No action is required on your part at this time.

2. [X] Please submit by __8/1/01__ a statement of your position with respect to the allegation(s) contained in this charge, with copies of any supporting documentation. This material will be made a part of the file and will be considered at the time that we investigate this charge. Your prompt response to this request will make it easier to conduct and conclude our investigation of this charge.

3. [ ] Please respond fully by _____ to the attached request for information which pertains to the allegations contained in this charge. Such information will be made a part of the file and will be considered by the Commission during the course of its investigation of the charge.

For further inquiry on this matter, please use the charge number shown above. Your position statement, your response to our request for information, or any inquiry you may have should be directed to:

Terry Mattoon
(Commission Representative)

555-4444
(Telephone Number)

[ ] Enclosure: Copy of Charge

BASIS OF DISCRIMINATION

[ ] RACE [ ] COLOR [X] SEX [ ] RELIGION [ ] NAT. ORIGIN [ ] AGE [ ] DISABILITY [ ] RETALIATION [ ] OTHER

CIRCUMSTANCES OF ALLEGED VIOLATION

Claimant states that she was denied partnership at the law firm of Parker & Gould because of her refusal to continue a sexual relationship with Simon Clark, a partner in the law firm of Parker & Gould. She further states that the law firm participated in the denial of partnership on that basis.

DATE	TYPED NAME/TITLE OF AUTHORIZED EEOC OFFICIAL	SIGNATURE
6/30/01	Terry Mattoon	*Terry Mattoon*

EEOC FORM 131 (Rev. 08/92)

CHARGING PARTY'S COPY

EXHIBIT 15

——— *PARKER & GOULD* ———
Four Independence Square
Nita City, Nita

September 1, 2001

Ms. Terry Mattoon
Equal Employment Opportunity
    Commission
22 Constitution Plaza
Nita City, Nita

Dear Ms. Mattoon:

I am writing on behalf of the law firm of Parker & Gould in
response to your correspondence of June 30, 2001, in which you
provided to us a Notice of Charge of Discrimination by Ms.
Margaret Polisi.

Parker & Gould categorically denies that the negative partnership decision by the firm concerning Ms. Polisi was on any
basis other than the merits. Ms. Polisi was denied partnership
in the firm because her billable hours were not acceptable,
the quality of her work was not acceptable, her ability to
attract business to the firm was not acceptable, and because
in times of personal crisis she was unable to adequately
perform her job functions at the firm.

If you have any further questions concerning this unfounded
allegation please feel free to contact me.

Sincerely,

Robert Bryant

Robert Bryant, Chair
Litigation Section

EXHIBIT 16

EQUAL EMPLOYMENT OPPORTUNITY COMMISSION
NOTICE OF RIGHT TO SUE
(Issued on request)

To:	From:
Ms. Margaret Polisi 7010 Greenhill Road Nita City, Nita ☐ *On behalf of a person aggrieved whose identity is CONFIDENTIAL (29 C.F.R. 1601.7(a))*	Equal Employment Opportunity Commission 22 Constitution Plaza Nita City, Nita

Charge Number	EEOC Representative	Telephone Number
2001-49985	Terry Mattoon	555-4444

(See the additional information attached to this form)

TO THE PERSON AGGRIEVED: This is your NOTICE OF RIGHT TO SUE. It is issued at your request. If you intend to sue the respondent(s) named in your charge, YOU MUST DO SO WITHIN NINETY (90) DAYS OF YOUR RECEIPT OF THIS NOTICE: OTHERWISE YOUR RIGHT TO SUE IS LOST.

☒ More than 180 days have expired since the filing of this charge.

☐ Less than 180 days have expired since the filing of this charge, but I have determined that the Commission will unable to complete its process within 180 days from the filing of the charge.

☒ With the issuance of this NOTICE OF RIGHT TO SUE, the Commission is terminating its process with respect to this charge.

☐ It has been determined that the Commission will continue to investigate your charge.

☐ ADEA: While Title VII and the ADA require EEOC to issue this notice of right to sue before you can bring a lawsuit you may sue under the Age Discrimination in Employment Act (ADEA) any time 60 days after your charge was filed until 90 days after you received notice that EEOC has completed action on your charge.

    ☐ Because EEOC is closing your case, your lawsuit under the ADEA must be brought within 90 days of your receipt of this notice. Otherwise, your right to sue is lost.

    ☐ EEOC is continuing its investigation. You will be notified when we have completed action and, if our notice will include notice of right to sue under the ADEA.

☐ EPA: While Title VII and the ADA require EEOC to issue this Notice of Right to Sue before you can bring a lawsuit you already have the right to sue under the Equal Pay Act (EPA) (You are not required to complain to any enforcement agency before bringing an EPA suit in court). EPA suits must be brought within 2 years (3 years for willful violations) of the alleged EPA underpayment.

I certify that this notice was mailed on the date set out below.

On Behalf of the Commission

___12/28/2001___
(Date Mailed)

___Terry Mattoon___

Enclosures
    Information Sheet
    Copy of Charge

cc: Respondents

EEOC Form 161-B (Test 10/94)

EXHIBIT 17

—— *PARKER & GOULD* ——
Four Independence Square
Nita City, Nita

October 15, 2001

Dean Martin Purcell
University of Nita
School of Law
One Campus Center
Nita City, Nita

Dear Marty,

It is with great pleasure that I write you concerning Ms. Margaret Polisi, who has applied for a teaching position at the law school. Over the past several years I have worked closely with her and feel well qualified to evaluate her abilities as a litigator, which I believe should translate over into the classroom.

Ms. Polisi came to us after a distinguished career at your school, where, as I am sure you know, she was an Editor of the Law Review and graduated first in her class. During her time at Parker & Gould she has worked on the most sophisticated of matters and has demonstrated enormous talent.

She possesses analytical prowess, a talent for precision and persuasiveness in writing, and the ability to articulate her clients' positions in effective oral advocacy. She has, quite frankly, excelled in all areas of lawyering.

In addition to her superb skills, Ms. Polisi has shown excellent maturity and does very well in client interaction. In fact, in a fairly recent case, involving one of our most sophisticated clients, she was commended by the client, in writing, at the successful conclusion of the case.

In closing, let me say that you will have a difficult time finding a better addition to your faculty than Ms. Polisi. If I can be of any further assistance, please to do not hesitate to call.

Please give my warmest regards to Ellen and the children.

Warm regards,

Simon Clark
Simon Clark

EXHIBIT 18

AFFIDAVIT OF JOHN RANDALL

My name is John Randall, and until recently I was a partner in the firm of Morrison & Farrow in Nita City. I have retired from the practice of law as of November 1, 2002 and will be moving to France to live in the near future. I do not intend to return to the United States any time in the near future.

I have agreed to give this affidavit before this court reporter and counsel for both the plaintiff and defendants in the case of <u>Polisi v. Clark and Parker & Gould</u> in order to tell what I know about the facts of this case.

In the summer of 2001 I received an impressive resume from an associate at Parker & Gould by the name of Margaret Polisi. I no longer have that resume but the document shown to me marked as Exhibit 1 looks familiar, although obviously, there were no job entries beyond her position at Parker & Gould. The resume also listed Simon Clark at P & G as a reference.

I have known Simon for over twenty years and I respect his opinion on legal talent, so I asked Ms. Polisi to have Simon send me a letter of recommendation. Shortly thereafter I received his letter of recommendation. Although the letter was not negative, I wouldn't call it a positive letter either. His evaluation of Ms. Polisi was apparently lukewarm. In addition, he included a handwritten note that I should take care regarding this candidate or something to that effect. Looking at what's been marked as Exhibit 11, that is the letter I received. The second handwritten note on the letter is in my handwriting.

When I received Simon's letter, I gave him a call and asked for an oral evaluation. He told me that Ms. Polisi had been turned down for partnership, a fact that I had assumed given her years at the firm, and the fact that she was applying for a job with us. He also told me that Ms. Polisi was not a good candidate for my practice, which was a white-collar-criminal practice, because there was reason to question her toughness and ability to cope with the stress inherent in my kind of practice. I then asked him whether she would be suitable for the civil litigation section of our firm where an opening had just occurred. He told me that in his opinion Ms. Polisi was not cut out for litigation of any sort, that she was just not reliable.

As a result of the letter and the phone call, I did not pursue hiring Ms. Polisi, nor did I refer her resume to the civil side of Morrison and Farrow.

Given her resume, absent the information from Simon Clark, we certainly would have interviewed Ms. Polisi for a position with our firm, on either the civil or criminal side. She seemed well qualified, at least on paper. Whether we would have hired her is an open question, and would have depended on her performance in the interview and whether we thought she would fit into the firm. Unlike P & G, we were then and are now a medium-sized law firm, so personality conflicts are a greater problem for us, and so the interview and our evaluation of how Ms. Polisi would fit in with the other men and women at the firm would have been an important consideration.

Further the affiant sayeth not.

John Randall

John Randall

Subscribed and sworn before me this 9th day of October, 2002.

Mary Williams

Mary Williams
Notary Public

JURY INSTRUCTIONS

1.   The court will now instruct you as to the claims and defenses of each party and the law governing the case. Please pay close attention to these instructions. You must arrive at your verdict by applying the law as you are now instructed to the facts as you find them.

2.   The parties to this case are Margaret Polisi, the plaintiff, and Simon Clark and the law firm of Parker & Gould, the co-defendants. Ms. Polisi has sued Mr. Clark and the law firm, seeking to recover damages based on a number of claims.

   a.   First, Ms. Polisi claims that Mr. Clark and the firm discriminated against her on the basis of her gender in violation of Title VII of the Civil Rights Act.

   On this gender discrimination claim, the plaintiff, Ms. Polisi, has the burden of proving, by a preponderance of the evidence, a *prima facie* case of discrimination. To do so, she must show: (1) she belongs to a protected class, i.e. she is a female, (2) she applied for a position with her employer (in this case, partnership in the law firm of Parker & Gould) which was available and for which she was qualified, (3) despite her qualifications, she was rejected for the position, and (4) after her rejection, the position remained open and her employer sought male applicants of plaintiff's qualifications.

   If Ms. Polisi succeeds in proving the prima facie case of gender discrimination, the burden shifts to the defendant(s) to articulate some legitimate, non-discriminatory reason for Ms. Polisi's rejection.

   Should the defendant(s) meet the burden of articulating a legitimate, non-discriminatory reason for rejecting Ms. Polisi for partnership in the law firm, the plaintiff, Ms. Polisi, must, then, prove, by a preponderance of the evidence, that the reasons offered by the defendant(s) were not the true reasons for her rejection, but rather a pretext for discrimination.

   b.   Second, the plaintiff, Ms. Polisi, claims that the defendants, Mr. Clark and the law firm of Parker & Gould, committed the act of *Quid Pro Quo* Gender Discrimination in violation of Title VII of the Civil Rights Act.

   In order to prevail on this claim, the Plaintiff, Ms. Polisi, must prove, by a preponderance of the evidence, that: (1) she was an employee of the defendant(s) and a female, (2) she was subjected to unwelcome sexual harassment in the form of sexual advances or requests for sexual favors, (3) the harassment complained of was based on sex, and (4) her submission to the unwelcomed advances was an express or implied condition for receiving job benefits or that the her refusal to submit to a supervisor's sexual demands resulted in tangible job detriment.

   Or Ms. Polisi must prove by a preponderance of the evidence, that (1) she was an employee of the defendant and a female (2) that she ended a voluntary sexual relationship with the defendant Clark; (3) that in retaliation of her actions the defendant Parker & Gould denied her a partnership in the firm and terminated her as an employee of the firm.

c.   Third, the plaintiff, Ms. Polisi, claims that the defendant(s), Mr. Clark and the law firm of Parker & Gould, committed the act of gender discrimination by creating a "hostile working environment," in violation of Title VII of the Civil Rights Act.

In order to prevail on this "hostile working environment" claim, the plaintiff, Ms. Polisi, must prove: (1) she was an employee and a member of a protected class, i.e. a female, (2) she was subjected to unwelcome sexual harassment, (3) the harassment complained of was based on sex, and (4) the harassment complained of affected a "term, condition or privilege" of employment in that it was sufficiently severe or pervasive to alter the condition of Ms. Polisi's employment and create an abusive working environment.

3.   If you find that Ms. Polisi has proved any or all of the above claims, you may award damages as follows:

a.   Award Ms. Polisi the amount of money in wages and fringe benefits which you determine Ms. Polisi lost as a result of defendant(s)' unlawful conduct from the date of her termination from Parker & Gould to the present with interest at the statutory rate, and

b.   Reinstate Ms. Polisi as a partner in the firm of Parker & Gould, or, in the alternative, award her "front pay" in the amount of wages and benefits which Ms. Polisi will lose in the future because of her unlawful termination from Parker & Gould.

c.   If you find that Ms. Polisi has proved none of the gender discrimination claims, you will render a verdict for the defendant(s) and award no damages.

4.   In addition to the above-mentioned claims of gender discrimination, Ms. Polisi also has sued the defendant(s), Simon Clark and Parker & Gould, seeking to recover damages for the tort of defamation.

In order to prevail on her claim of defamation, the plaintiff, Ms. Polisi, must prove, by a preponderance of the evidence, that the defendant(s) published at least one statement which defamed her, causing her harm.

"Publication" means that the defendant(s) communicated by speaking or writing an idea to some other person.

A communication is "defamatory" if, taken as a whole, it tends to harm the reputation of the victim as to lower her in the estimation of the community or to deter a third party from associating or dealing with her.

If you find that the communication, even if it was defamatory of the plaintiff, was substantially true, you will return a verdict in favor of the defendant(s) and against the plaintiff.

If you find that the defendant(s)' communication was defamatory, but was made subject to a conditional privilege, then you must find for the defendant(s) unless the plaintiff proves that the privilege was abused by the defendant(s) in that they acted knowingly, recklessly or maliciously.

In this case, I find and instruct you a conditional privilege applies. This privilege conditionally protects statements made where the publisher(s) of the statement (the defendant(s)) reasonably believe(s) that he or she is protecting the interest of the recipient of the statement or a person who may act on the defamatory statement. For example, the conditional statement extends to statements of reference made by an employer about a present or past employee to a prospective employer. Thus, the references provided by Simon Clark to Margaret Polisi's prospective employers are within the protection of the conditional privilege.

However, you shall find that the defendant(s) lost the protection of the privilege if the plaintiff proves, by a preponderance of the evidence, that the defendant(s) defamed her with knowledge of its falsity, recklessly (that is, without regard to whether it was true or false), or intentionally.

If you find that the defendant(s) are liable for defamation, the plaintiff is entitled to be fairly and adequately compensated for all harm she suffered as a result of the defamatory communications published by the defendant(s). The injuries for which you may compensate the plaintiff by an award of damages against the defendant(s) include:

a.   the actual harm to the plaintiff's reputation which you find resulted from the defendant(s) conduct, and

b.   the emotional distress, mental anguish, and humiliation which you find the plaintiff suffered as a result of the defendant(s)' conduct (as well as the bodily harm which you find was caused by such suffering).

5.   Special Instruction on Agency.

A principal is liable for the acts of its agent if the agent is liable, where: (1) a principal-agent relationship exists, and (2) the agent performs the acts for which he is liable while acting within the scope of his employment and in furtherance of the principal's business. I instruct you that defendant Simon Clark was, at all times material to this lawsuit, the agent of the defendant Parker & Gould, and was at all times acting within the scope of his employment with Parker & Gould. Thus, all conduct performed by Simon Clark is the responsibility not only of Simon Clark, but of Parker & Gould.

IN THE UNITED STATES DISTRICT COURT
FOR THE DISTRICT OF NITA

MARGARET POLISI   :
                         :
        Plaintiff   :   CIVIL ACTION NO.
                         :   2002-4678
        v.   :
                         :
                         :   JURY TRIAL DEMANDED
                         :
SIMON CLARK   :
                         :
        and   :
                         :
PARKER & GOULD   :
                         :
        Defendants   :

SPECIAL VERDICT FORM

We, the jury, and each of us, finds:

1.   (a) On Claim I, for the Plaintiff in the amount of

     $_____.

     (b) On Claim I, for the Defendant(s).

     (Answer either Question 1(a) or 1(b).)

2.   (a) On Claim II, for the Plaintiff in the amount of

     $_____.

     (b) On Claim II, for the Defendant(s)

     (Answer either Question 2(a) or 2(b).)

3. (a) On Claim III, for the Plaintiff in the amount of

$_____.

(b) On Claim III, for the Defendants.

(Answer either Question 3(a) or 3(b).)

4. (a) On Claim IV, for the Plaintiff in the amount of

$_____.

(b) On Claim IV, for the Defendants.

(Answer either Question 4(a) or 4(b).)

_____
Foreperson

Blank Slide   **Slide 1**

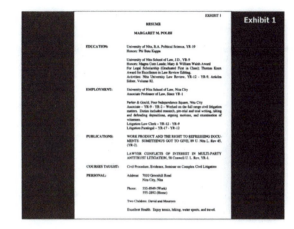

Exhibit 1   **Slide 2**

Exhibit 1   **Slide 3**

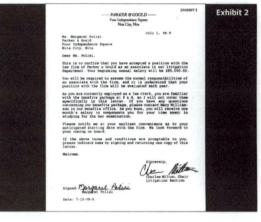

Exhibit 2   **Slide 4**

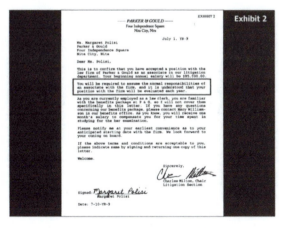

Exhibit 2   **Slide 5**

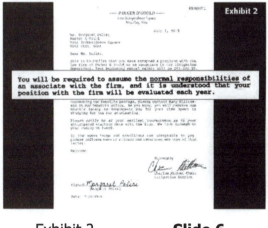

Exhibit 2   **Slide 6**

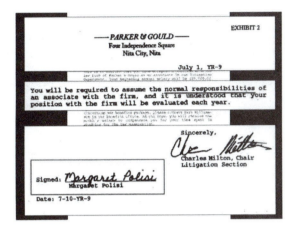

Exhibit 2   **Slide 7**

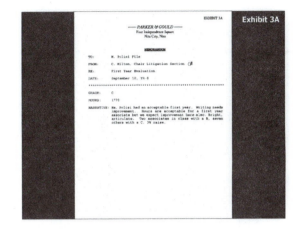

Exhibit 3A   **Slide 8**

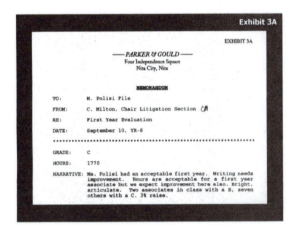

Exhibit 3A   **Slide 9**

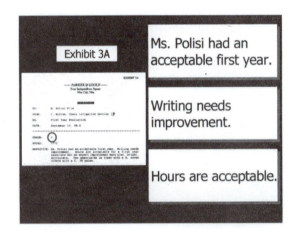

Exhibit 3A   **Slide 10**

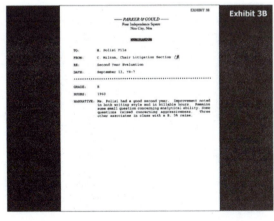

Exhibit 3B   **Slide 11**

Exhibit 3B   **Slide 12**

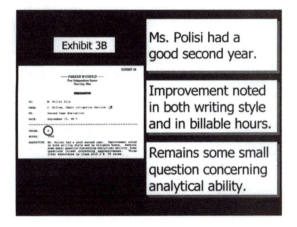

Exhibit 3B

Ms. Polisi had a good second year.

Improvement noted in both writing style and in billable hours.

Remains some small question concerning analytical ability.

Exhibit 3B   **Slide 13**

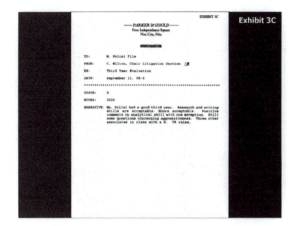

Exhibit 3C   **Slide 14**

Exhibit 3C   **Slide 15**

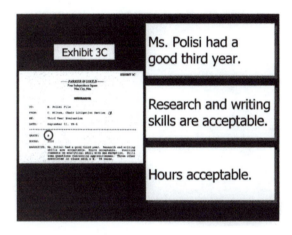

Ms. Polisi had a good third year.

Research and writing skills are acceptable.

Hours acceptable.

Exhibit 3C   **Slide 16**

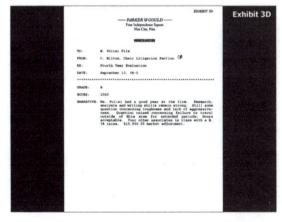

Exhibit 3D   **Slide 17**

Exhibit 3D   **Slide 18**

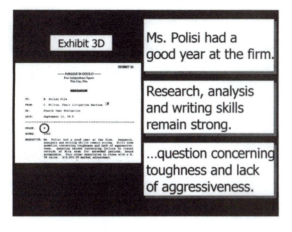

Exhibit 3D

Slide 19

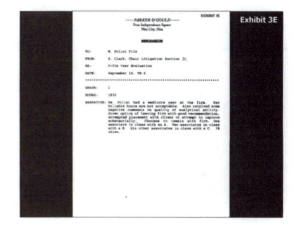

Exhibit 3E

Slide 20

Exhibit 3E

Slide 21

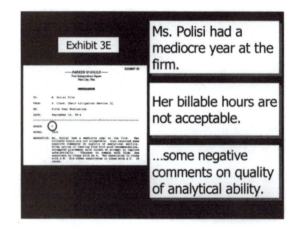

Exhibit 3E

Slide 22

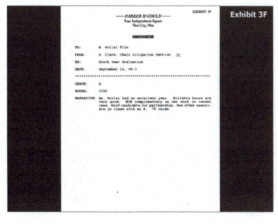

Exhibit 3F

Slide 23

Exhibit 3F

Slide 24

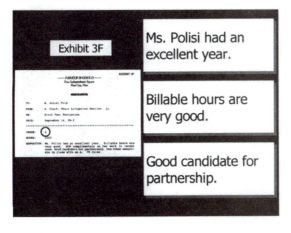

Exhibit 3F   **Slide 25**

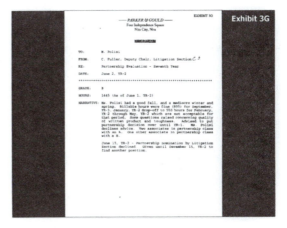

Exhibit 3G   **Slide 26**

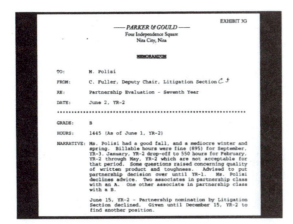

Exhibit 3G   **Slide 27**

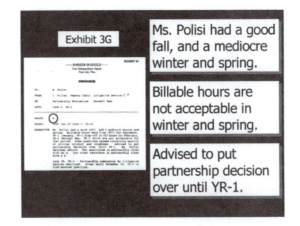

Exhibit 3G   **Slide 28**

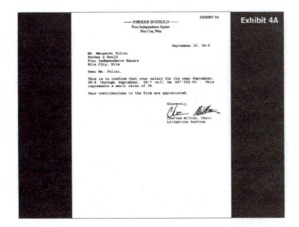

Exhibit 4A   **Slide 29**

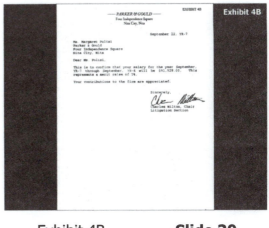

Exhibit 4B   **Slide 30**

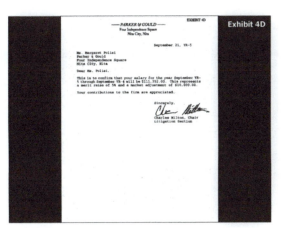

Exhibit 4C   **Slide 31**

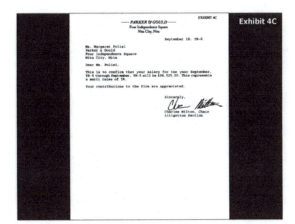

Exhibit 4D   **Slide 32**

Exhibit 4E   **Slide 33**

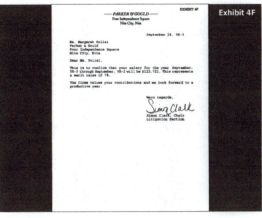

Exhibit 4F   **Slide 34**

Exhibit 4F   **Slide 35**

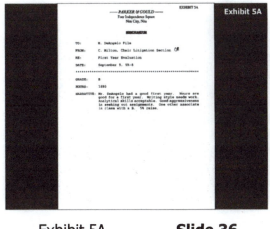

Exhibit 5A   **Slide 36**

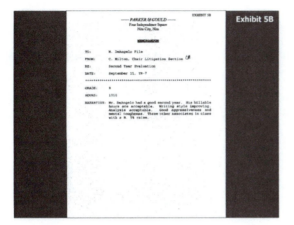

Exhibit 5B   **Slide 37**

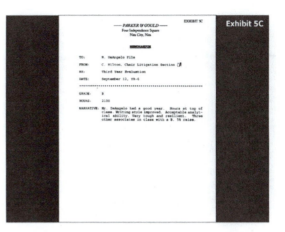

Exhibit 5C   **Slide 38**

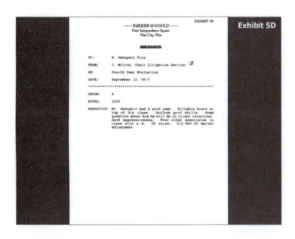

Exhibit 5D   **Slide 39**

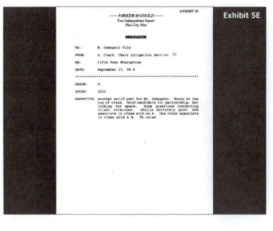

Exhibit 5E   **Slide 40**

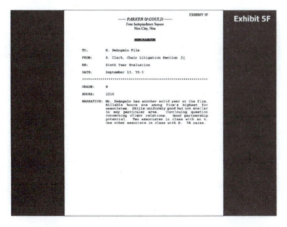

Exhibit 5F   **Slide 41**

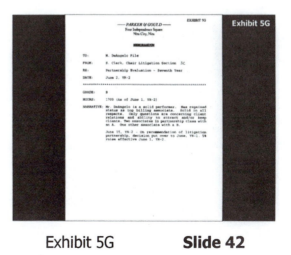

Exhibit 5G   **Slide 42**

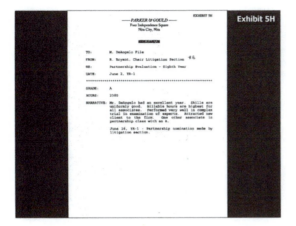

Exhibit 5H   **Slide 43**

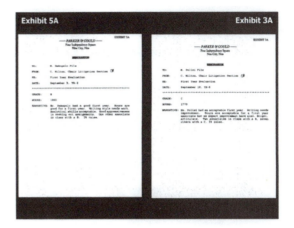

Exhibit 5A & 3A   **Slide 44**

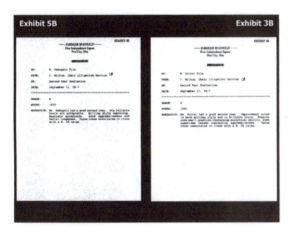

Exhibit 5B & 3B   **Slide 45**

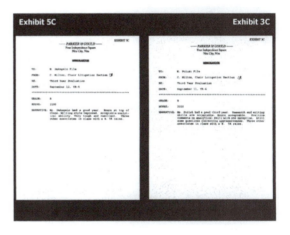

Exhibit 5C & 3C   **Slide 46**

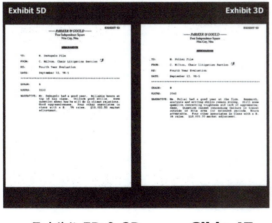

Exhibit 5D & 3D   **Slide 47**

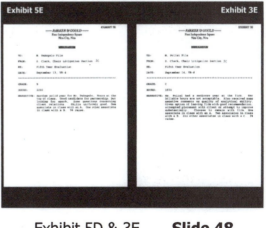

Exhibit 5D & 3E   **Slide 48**

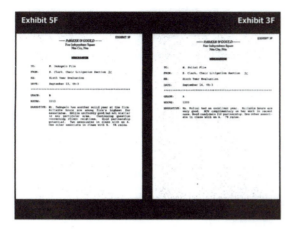

Exhibit 5F & 3F   **Slide 49**

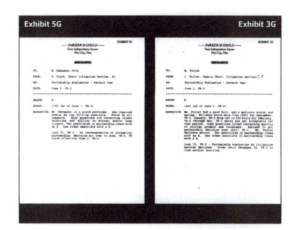

Exhibit 5G & 3G   **Slide 50**

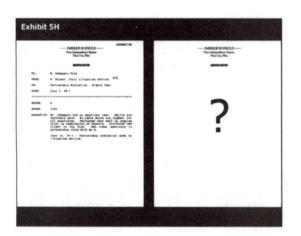

Exhibit 5H & ?   **Slide 51**

Exhibit 6   **Slide 52**

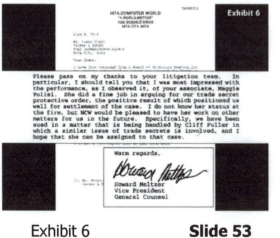

Exhibit 6   **Slide 53**

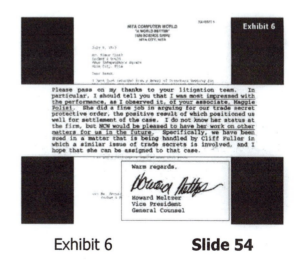

Exhibit 6   **Slide 54**

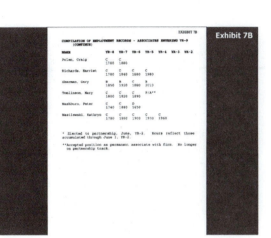

Exhibit 7A | **Slide 55**

Exhibit 7B | **Slide 56**

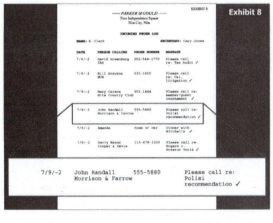

Exhibit 7 | **Slide 57**

Exhibit 8 | **Slide 58**

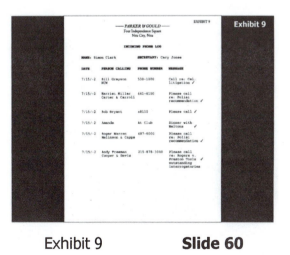

Exhibit 8 | **Slide 59**

Exhibit 9 | **Slide 60**

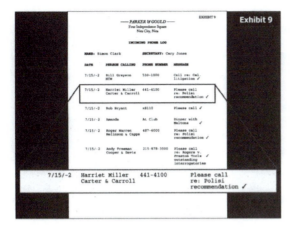

Exhibit 9   **Slide 61**

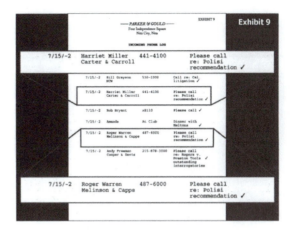

Exhibit 9   **Slide 62**

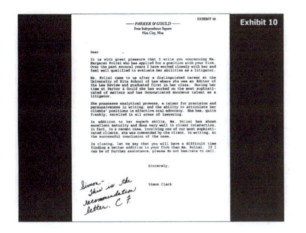

Exhibit 10   **Slide 63**

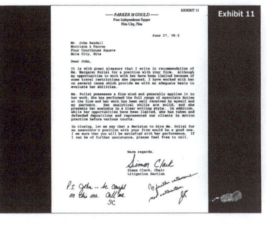

Exhibit 11   **Slide 64**

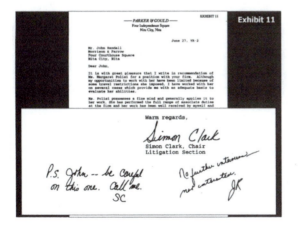

Exhibit 11   **Slide 65**

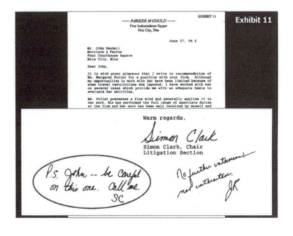

Exhibit 11   **Slide 66**

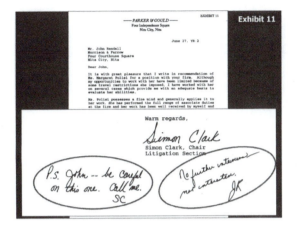

Exhibit 11   **Slide 67**

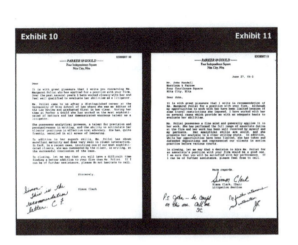

Exhibit 10 & 11   **Slide 68**

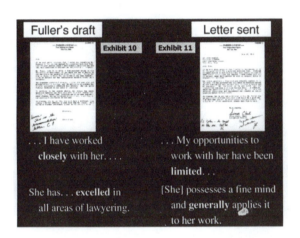

Exhibit 10 & 11   **Slide 69**

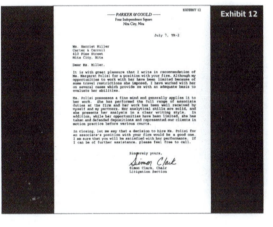

Exhibit 12   **Slide 70**

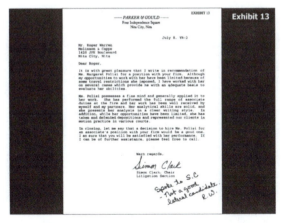

Exhibit 13   **Slide 71**

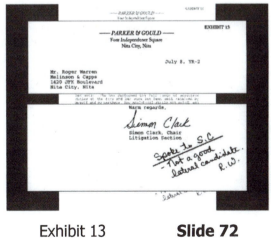

Exhibit 13   **Slide 72**

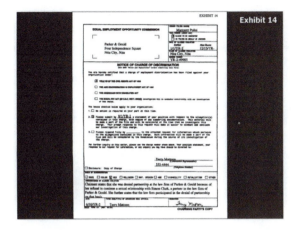

Exhibit 14   **Slide 73**

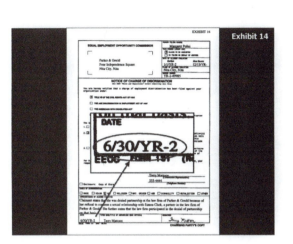

Exhibit 14   **Slide 74**

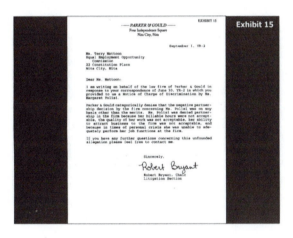

Exhibit 15   **Slide 75**

Exhibit 15   **Slide 76**

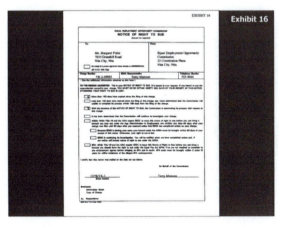

Exhibit 16   **Slide 77**

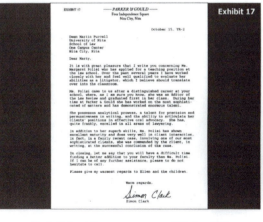

Exhibit 17   **Slide 78**

Exhibit 10 & 17   **Slide 79**

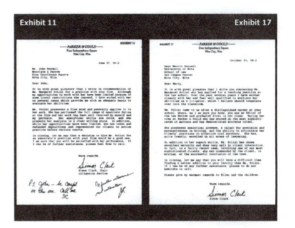

Exhibit 11 & 17   **Slide 80**

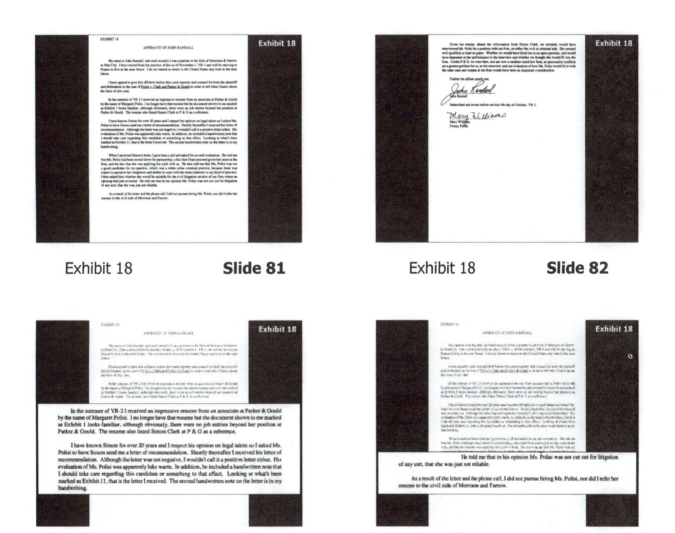

Exhibit 18   **Slide 81**

Exhibit 18   **Slide 82**

In the summer of YR-2 I received an impressive resume from an associate at Parker & Gould by the name of Margaret Polisi. I no longer have that resume but the document shown to me marked as Exhibit 1 looks familiar, although obviously, there were no job entries beyond her position at Parker & Gould. The resume also listed Simon Clark at P & G as a reference.

I have known Simon for over 20 years and I respect his opinion on legal talent so I asked Ms. Polisi to have Simon send me a letter of recommendation. Although the letter was not negative, I wouldn't call it a positive letter either. His evaluation of Ms. Polisi was apparently luke warm. In addition, he included a handwritten note that I should take care regarding this candidate or something to that effect. Looking at what's been marked as Exhibit 11, that is the letter I received. The second handwritten note on the letter is in my handwriting.

Exhibit 18   **Slide 83**

He told me that in his opinion Ms. Polisi was not cut out for litigation of any sort, that she was just not reliable.

As a result of the letter and the phone call, I did not pursue hiring Ms. Polisi, nor did I refer her resume to the civil side of Morrison and Farrow.

Exhibit 18   **Slide 84**

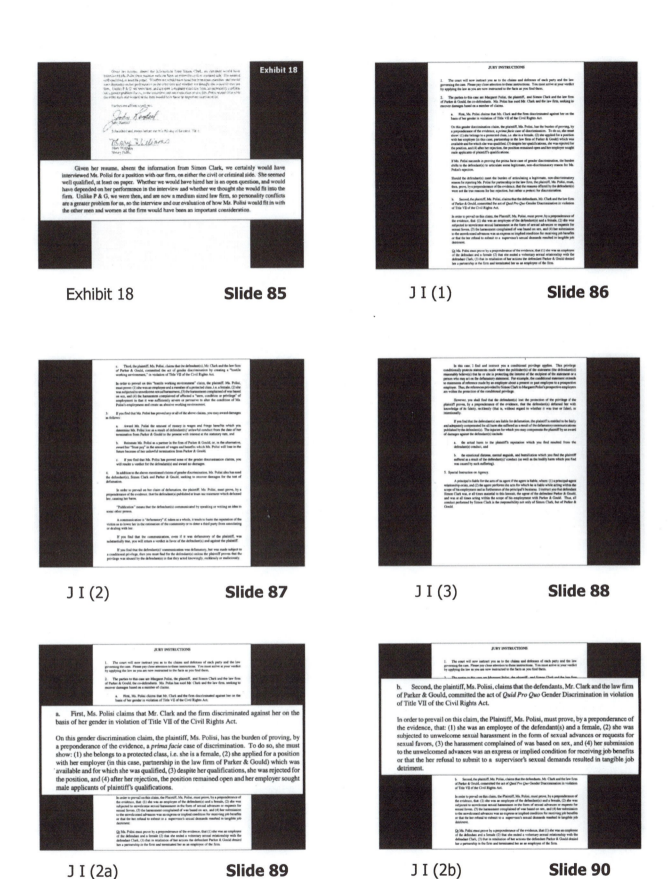

Exhibit 18   **Slide 85**

J I (1)   **Slide 86**

J I (2)   **Slide 87**

J I (3)   **Slide 88**

J I (2a)   **Slide 89**

J I (2b)   **Slide 90**

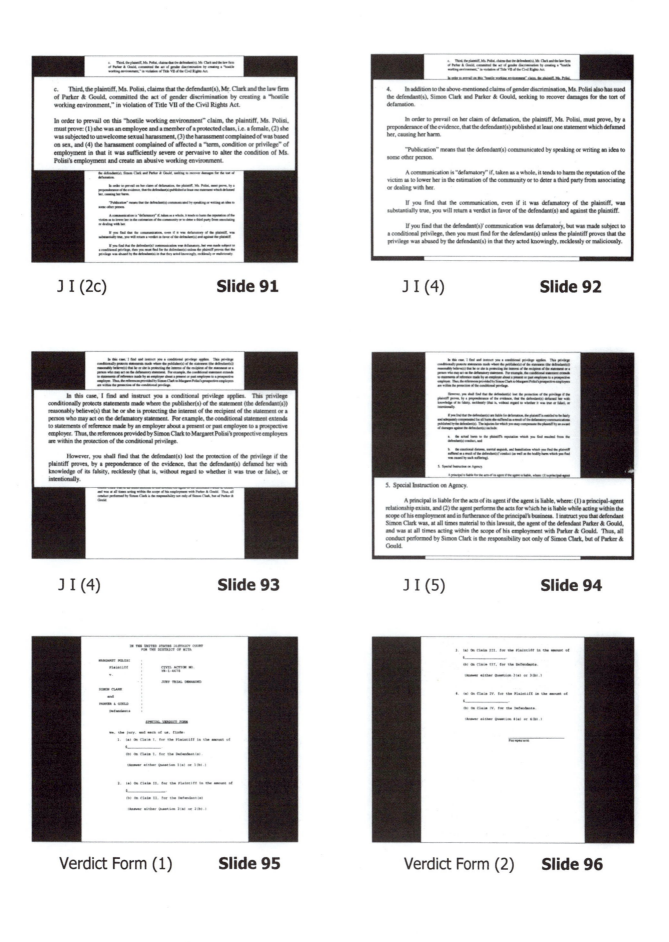

J I (2c)　　　　　　　**Slide 91**

J I (4)　　　　　　　**Slide 92**

J I (4)　　　　　　　**Slide 93**

J I (5)　　　　　　　**Slide 94**

Verdict Form (1)　　　**Slide 95**

Verdict Form (2)　　　**Slide 96**

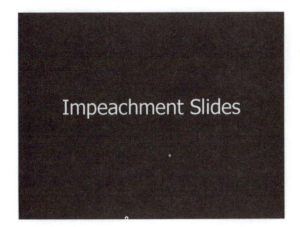

Slide 97

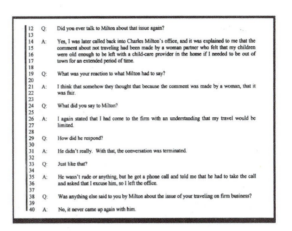

MP p. 20, L 12–40 **Slide 98**

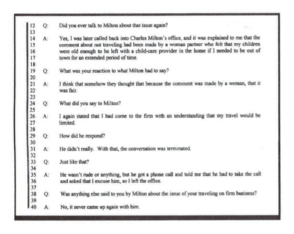

MP p. 20, L 12–40 **Slide 99**

Video MP **Slide 100**

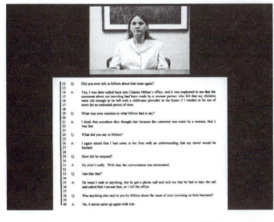

Video w trans **Slide 101**

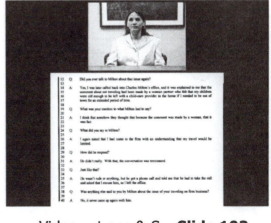

Video w trans & S **Slide 102**

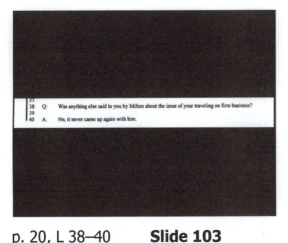

Q: Was anything else said to you by Milton about the issue of your traveling on firm business?
A: No, it never came up again with him.

p. 20, L 38–40 **Slide 103**

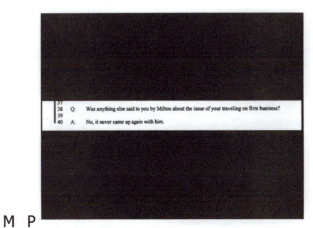

M P

Q: Was anything else said to you by Milton about the issue of your traveling on firm business?
A: No, it never came up again with him.

MP p. 20, L 38–40 S **Slide 104**

Video MP **Slide 105**

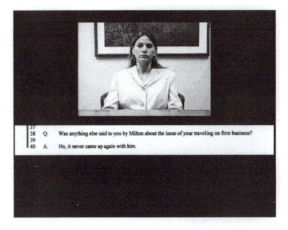

Q: Was anything else said to you by Milton about the issue of your traveling on firm business?
A: No, it never came up again with him.

Video w trans **Slide 106**

Q: Was anything else said to you by Milton about the issue of your traveling on firm business?
A: No, it never came up again with him.

Video w trans & S **Slide 107**

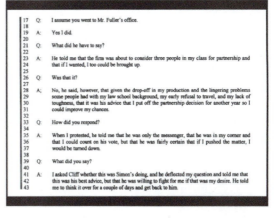

MP p. 27, L 17–43 **Slide 108**

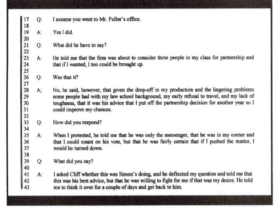

MP p. 27, L 17–43 S   **Slide 109**

Video MP   **Slide 110**

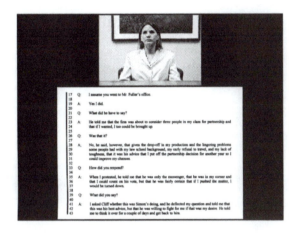

Video w trans   **Slide 111**

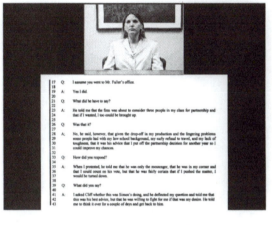

Video w trans S   **Slide 112**

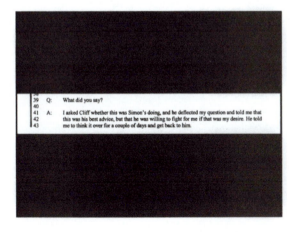

MP p. 27, L 39–43   **Slide 113**

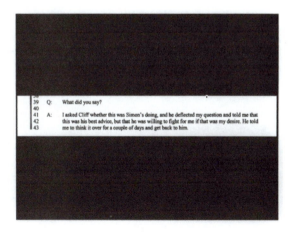

MP p. 27, L 39–43 S   **Slide 114**

Video MP   **Slide 115**

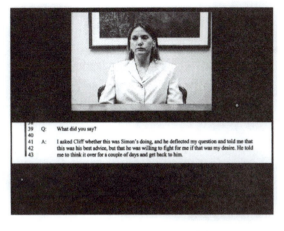

Video w trans   **Slide 116**

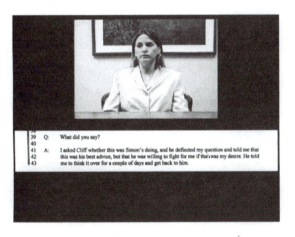

Video w trans & S   **Slide 117**

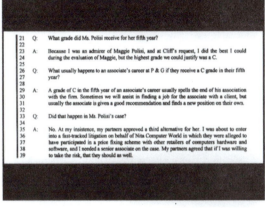

SC p. 56, L 21–39   **Slide 118**

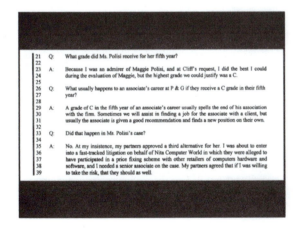

SC p. 56, L 21–39 S   **Slide 119**

Video SC   **Slide 120**

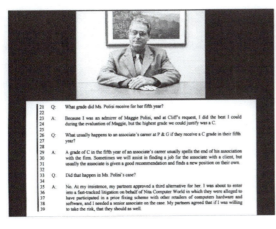

Video w trans   **Slide 121**

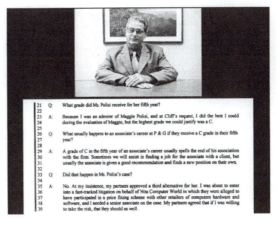

Video w trans & S   **Slide 122**

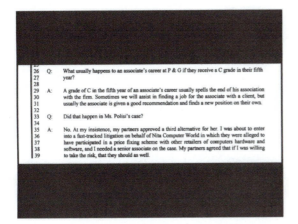

SC p. 56, L 26–39   **Slide 123**

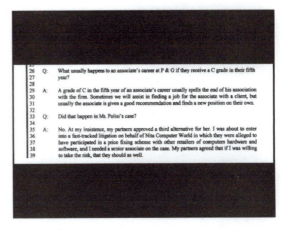

SC p. 56, L 26–39 S   **Slide 124**

Video SC   **Slide 125**

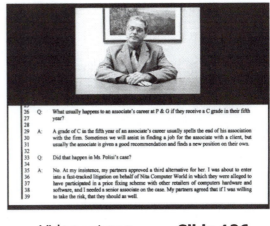

Video w trans   **Slide 126**

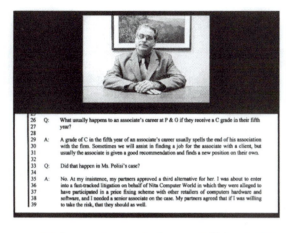

Video w trans & S **Slide 127**

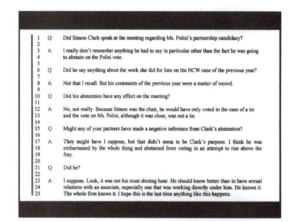

JP p. 67, L 1–25 **Slide 128**

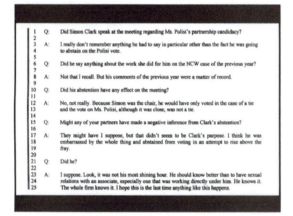

JP p. 67, L 1–25 S **Slide 129**

Video JP **Slide 130**

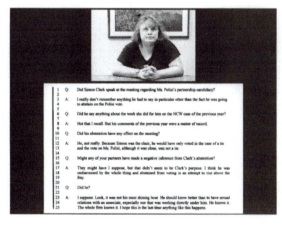

Video w trans **Slide 131**

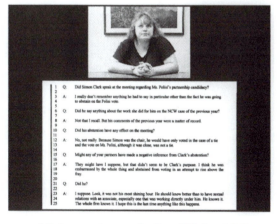

Video w trans & S **Slide 132**

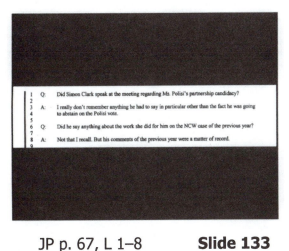

JP p. 67, L 1–8 **Slide 133**

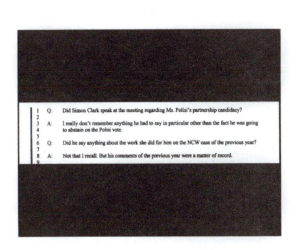

JP p. 67, L 1–8 S **Slide 134**

Video JP **Slide 135**

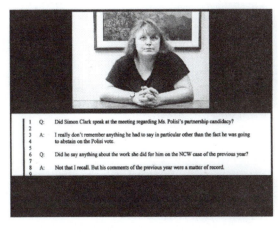

Video w trans **Slide 136**

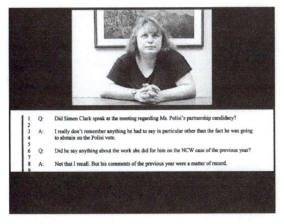

Video w trans & S **Slide 137**

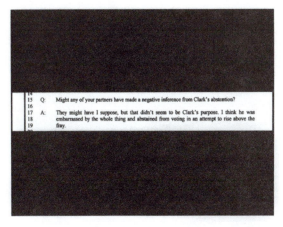

JP p. 67, L 15–19 **Slide 138**

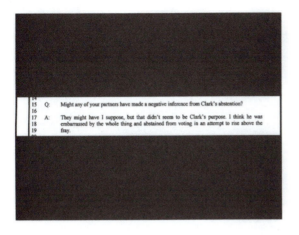

JP p. 67, L 15–19 S   **Slide 139**

Video JP   **Slide 140**

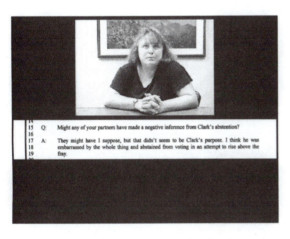

Video w trans   **Slide 141**

Video w trans & S   **Slide 142**

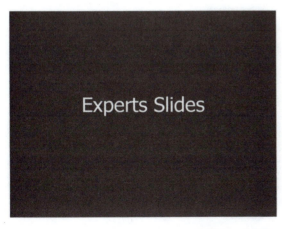

Experts Slides

Slide 143

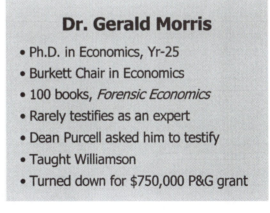

Dr. Gerald Morris

- Ph.D. in Economics, Yr-25
- Burkett Chair in Economics
- 100 books, *Forensic Economics*
- Rarely testifies as an expert
- Dean Purcell asked him to testify
- Taught Williamson
- Turned down for $750,000 P&G grant

Morris   **Slide 144**

Morris's Assumptions

- Absent discrimination, would have made partner at P&G in Yr-2
- Median & Mean partner earning data @ P&G
- Future earnings increase of 6.61%
- Discount rate of 5%
- Under defamation, associate at other firm until 1/1/YR+2, then promoted to partner

Morris Assumptions   **Slide 145**

Law school wages Assumptions

- P&G associate wage from 6/1/Yr-2 to 12/31/Yr-2
- Starts Nita as adjunct in Spring Yr-1
- Goes tenure track 9/Yr-1
- Full professor as of Yr+7
- Average annual full professor salary of $95,000 (taken from Nita U data)

Law Assumptions   **Slide 146**

What Maggie would have earned at P&G

Past Earnings (Yr-2 to Yr-0)	$ 359,861
Future Earnings (Yr+1 to Yr+24)	13,328,480
Lost P&G Earnings	**$13,688,341**

What Maggie   **Slide 147**

Losses due to Discrimination

Earnings Absent Discrimination	$13,688,341
Less Mitigated Earnings (as Prof)	2,850,009
Total Economic Loss	**$10,838,332**

Losses Discrimination **Slide 148**

What Polisi would have earned at another firm (discrimination)

Past Earnings (Yr-1 to Yr-0)	$ 253,861
Future Earnings (Yr+1 to Yr+24)	7,192,979
Total Earnings	**$7,446,840**

What Polisi   **Slide 149**

Losses due to Defamation

Earnings Absent Defamation	$7,446,840
Less Mitigated Earnings	2,850,009
Total Economic Loss	**$4,596,831**

Losses Defamation **Slide 150**

Dr. Denise Williamson

- Ph.D. at Nita University, Yr-16
- Forensic Economics, Ltd.
- Litigation support for law firms
- Expert for defense 95% of time
- Hired by P&G 26 times
- Average fee = $9,000 - $10,000 per case

Williamson   **Slide 151**

Williamson's Assumptions

- Re: discrimination, if made P&G partner, only non-equity partner
- If only defamation, then only an associate at P&G or at another firm
- Discount rate of 7.5%
- Never calculates assuming full partnership

Williamson Asmpt   **Slide 152**

Alternative wage assumption #1: Nita Computer World

- Would have started at $120,000
- Uses data provided by Fuller at NCW
- Pre-Yr+7 earnings at NCW more than long-term associate
- By Yr+7 earnings at NCW as much as non-equity partner at P&G, and greater than long-term associate
- Therefore: no economic loss

Alternative wage 1   **Slide 153**

Alternative wage assumption #2: Law School

- Took position as adjunct professor in Spring Yr-1 at $75,000/year
- Tenure track in 9/Yr-1
- Full professor Yr+7, salary of $125,000
- Uses P&G associate salary from 6/1 to 12/31 Yr-2 of $122,721
- Therefore: loss = $0 to $305,696

Alternative wage 2   **Slide 154**

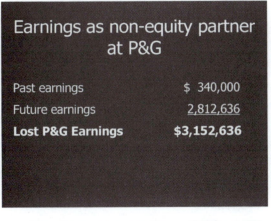

Earnings as non-equity partner at P&G

Past earnings	$ 340,000
Future earnings	2,812,636
Lost P&G Earnings	**$3,152,636**

Earnings non-equity   **Slide 155**

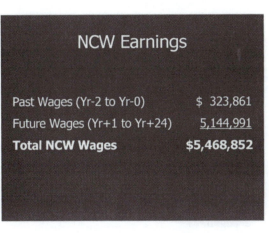

NCW Earnings

Past Wages (Yr-2 to Yr-0)	$ 323,861
Future Wages (Yr+1 to Yr+24)	5,144,991
Total NCW Wages	**$5,468,852**

NCW earnings   **Slide 156**

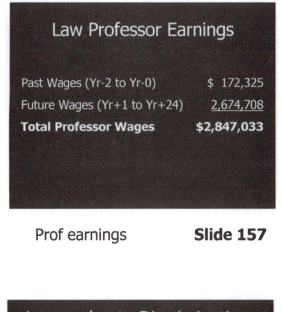

Law Professor Earnings

Past Wages (Yr-2 to Yr-0)	$ 172,325
Future Wages (Yr+1 to Yr+24)	2,674,708
Total Professor Wages	**$2,847,033**

Prof earnings **Slide 157**

Loss due to Discrimination: NCW Mitigation

Earnings Absent Discrimination	$3,152,636
Less NCW Compensation	5,468,851
Loss at NCW	**-0-**

Loss discrim NCW **Slide 158**

Losses due to Discrimination: Law Professor Mitigation

Earnings Absent Discrimination	$3,152,636
Less Earnings as Law Professor	2,846,942
Loss as Professor	**$ 305,694**

Loss discrim prof **Slide 159**

Earnings as senior associate [used in defamation calculations]

Past Wages (Yr-2 to Yr-0)	$ 327,067
Future Wages (Yr+1 to Yr+24)	2,375,323
Total Associate Earnings	**$ 2,702,390**

Earnings **Slide 160**

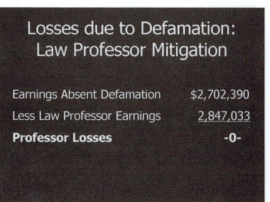

Losses due to Defamation: Law Professor Mitigation

Earnings Absent Defamation	$2,702,390
Less Law Professor Earnings	2,847,033
Professor Losses	**-0-**

Loss def prof **Slide 161**

Losses due to Defamation: NCW Mitigation

Earnings Absent Discrimination	$2,702,391
Less NCW Wages	5,468,851
NCW Losses	**-0-**

Loss def NCW **Slide 162**

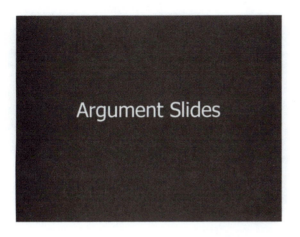

Argument Slides

Slide 163

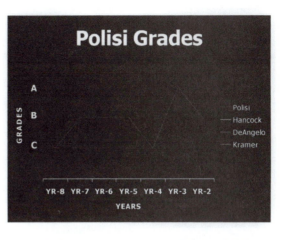

Polisi grades   **Slide 164**

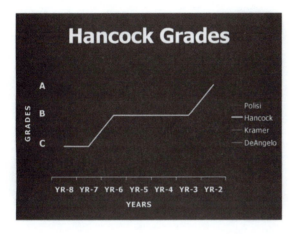

Hancock grades   **Slide 165**

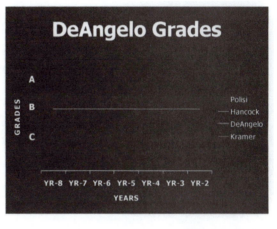

DeAngelo grades   **Slide 166**

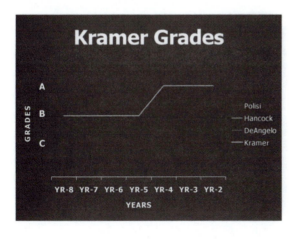

Kramer grades   **Slide 167**

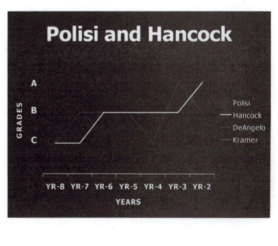

Polisi & Hancock   **Slide 168**

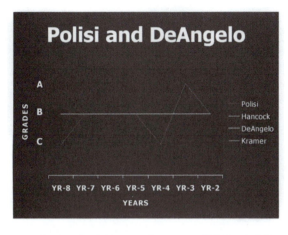

Polisi & DeAngelo   **Slide 169**

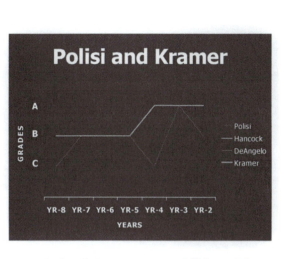

Polisi & Kramer   **Slide 170**

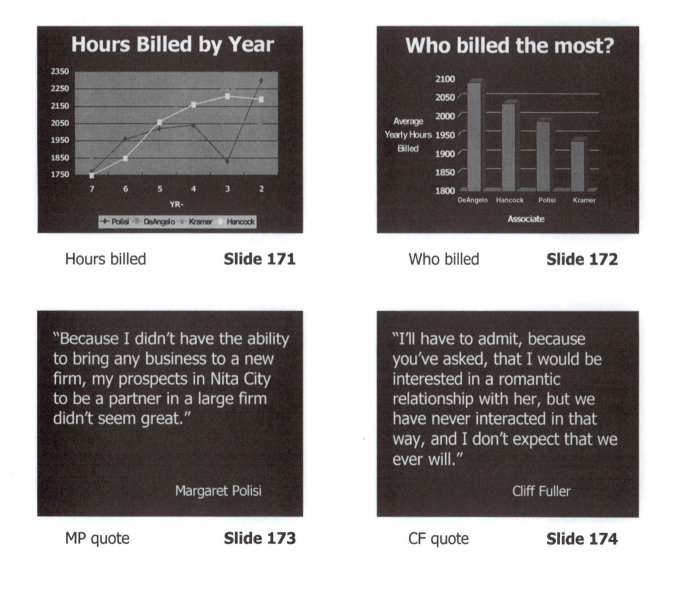

Hours billed   **Slide 171**

Who billed   **Slide 172**

"Because I didn't have the ability to bring any business to a new firm, my prospects in Nita City to be a partner in a large firm didn't seem great."

Margaret Polisi

MP quote   **Slide 173**

"I'll have to admit, because you've asked, that I would be interested in a romantic relationship with her, but we have never interacted in that way, and I don't expect that we ever will."

Cliff Fuller

CF quote   **Slide 174**

"I had had approximately ten extramarital relationships with women who were or are employees of P & G. To be honest I cannot remember all of their names..."

Simon Clark

SC quote   **Slide 175**

"If a choice had to be made between Ms. Polisi and Simon Clark, and it did not happen here in my opinion, the only correct decision would be in favor of Simon Clark."

Jayne Post

JP quote   **Slide 176**

"Look, it was not his most shining hour. He should know better than to have sexual relations with an associate, especially one that was working under him. He knows it. The whole firm knows it."

Jayne Post

JP quote   **Slide 177**

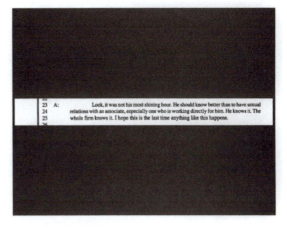

JP quote   **Slide 178**

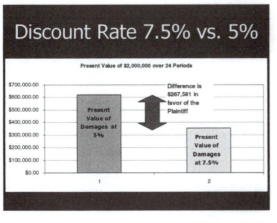

Discount rate   **Slide 179**

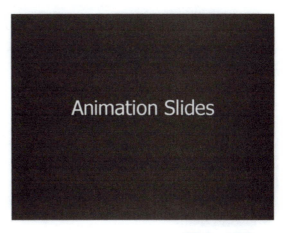

Animation Slides

                            Slide 180

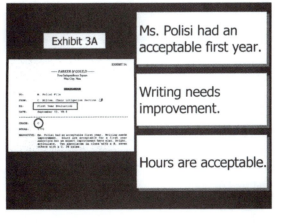

Exhibit 3A

Slide 181

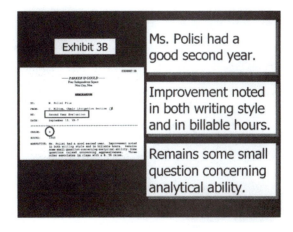

Exhibit 3B

Slide 182

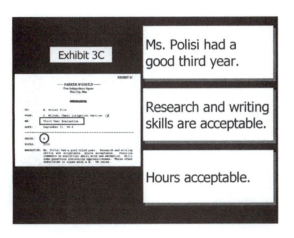

Exhibit 3C

Slide 183

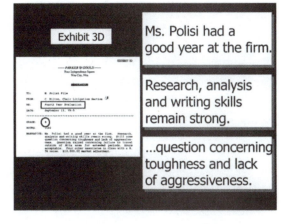

Exhibit 3D

Slide 184

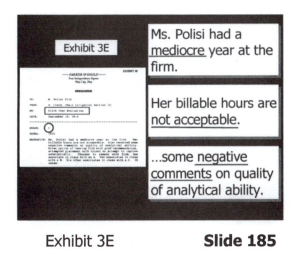

Exhibit 3E

Slide 185

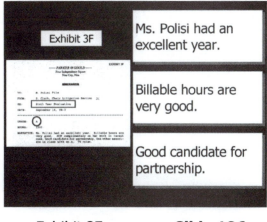

Exhibit 3F

Slide 186

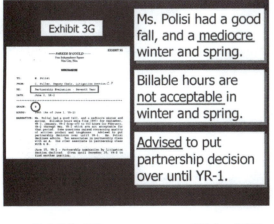

Exhibit 3G   **Slide 187**

Polisi grades   **Slide 188**

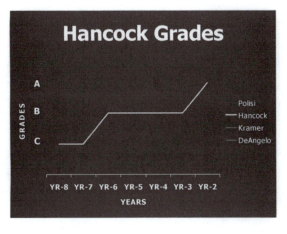

Hancock grades   **Slide 189**

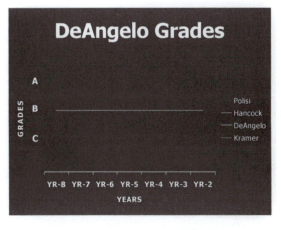

DeAngelo grades   **Slide 190**

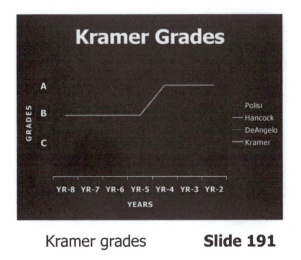

Kramer grades   **Slide 191**

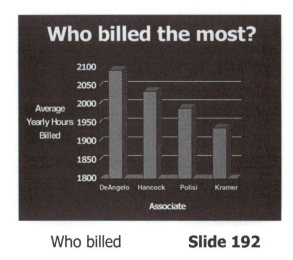

Who billed   **Slide 192**

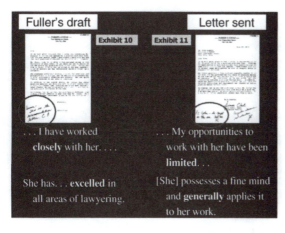

Exhibit 10 & 11   **Slide 193**

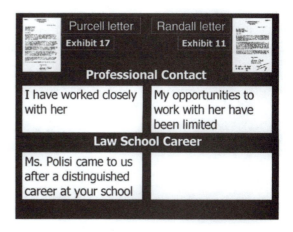

Exhibit 17 &11   **Slide 194**

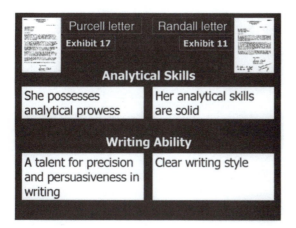

Exhibit 17 & 11   **Slide 195**

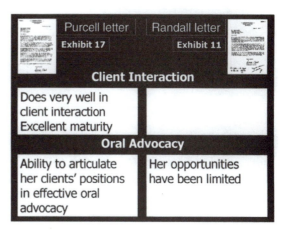

Exhibit 17 & 11   **Slide 196**

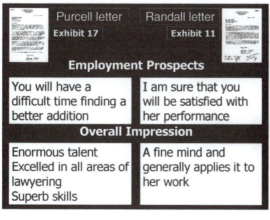

Exhibit 17 & 11   **Slide 197**

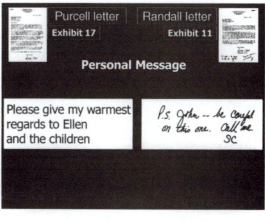

Exhibit 17 & 11   **Slide 198**

Clark to Purcell	Clark to Randall
worked closely with her	limited opportunities
a distinguished career	
analytical prowess	analytical skills are solid
talent for precision	clear writing style
ability to articulate	opportunities limited
excellent maturity	
difficult time finding a better addition	will be satisfied with her performance
enormous talent, excelled, superb skills	fine mind and generally applies it to her work

Clark to   **Slide 199**

A done deal   **Slide 200**

"You're all the same."

"You don't know when you have a good thing going."

"You'll regret this, I promise you."

SC quote   **Slide 201**

JP video p. 67, 23–25   **Slide 202**

SPECIAL IMPEACHMENT PROBLEMS
(To Be Used in Conjunction With Slides 97–142)

1. Assume that Margaret Polisi testified on her own behalf on direct examination. During that examination she was asked questions about her evaluation meeting with Charles Milton during which her failure to travel was raised as a negative in her evaluation. Assume that Ms. Polisi testified consistent with her deposition on page 20 with the following exception:

    Q: So you never heard again from Milton about the issue of failure to travel?

    A: Now that you mention it, I did hear again from him. Several days after our follow-up conversation that ended abruptly he called me and apologized for not finishing our conversation. He then said that he had spoken to people on the hiring committee and that of course the firm would live up to its commitment about not requiring me to travel and that in no way would it ever be considered against me. That was good enough for me.

For the Defendant, impeachment the testimony of Polisi regarding this testimony utilizing the written or video transcript of her deposition, or both.

2. Assume that Margaret Polisi testified on her own behalf on direct examination. During that examination she testified about the meeting she had before her partnership decision with Cliff Fuller in which Fuller recommended that she put the decision off a year. Assume that Ms. Polisi testified consistent with her testimony on page 27 with the following exception:

    "I asked Cliff if Simon was behind my negative evaluation and he left the very clear impression that he was. Cliff said, "I'll do my best for you but you know I don't have the power that other interested parties have, so I'm not optimistic." Who else could he have been talking about other than Simon. I had no other real enemies in the firm, except for Jayne Post, perhaps, but she was hardly considered a powerful person in the firm."

For the Defendant, impeach the testimony of Polisi regarding this testimony utilizing the written or video transcript of her deposition, or both.

3. Assume that Simon Clark has testified on his own behalf on direct examination. During that examination, he testified as to the events surrounding Polisi's fifth year evaluation and when she came to work with him on the NCW case. Assume that Clark testified consistent with his testimony on page 56 with the following exception:

    Q: Whose decision was it to allow Ms. Polisi to work on the NCW case and redeem her bad fifth year.

    A: In the end it was the partnership's decision, but they wouldn't have done so without my consent. It was against my better judgment to allow this, not because of Maggie because I believed that she was a talented lawyer who got caught in some bad circumstances, but because it was bad policy to ignore our tradition. I never informed the partnership of this but at the end of the day, I agreed to her working on the NCW case only after some high powered lobbying by Cliff Fuller, who was Maggie's strongest supporter. Cliff and I were very close and he asked me for that favor and I gave it to him. When I asked that the partnership allow Ms. Polisi this other alternative they were kind enough to agree and in fact, she turned out to do a great job in the case.

For the Plaintiff, impeach the testimony of Clark utilizing the written or video transcript of his deposition, or both.

4. Assume that Jayne Post has testified on behalf of the Defendants on direct examination. During that examination she testified about the meeting during which Polisi's nomination for partnership was declined. She testified consistent with her testimony on page 67 with the following exception.

> "Simon was not as active in Polisi's meeting as normal. He did speak about the fine job she had done for NCW and made no negative comments regarding her performance as a lawyer whatsoever. With regard to the abstention, I don't know how anyone could have taken that as a negative for Polisi, or a sign that Simon was opposed to her nomination; especially as he was favorable towards her in his direct comments. To the contrary, if someone were looking for a hidden meaning it would more likely be that Simon was saying, "I can't vote for her because of my personal relationship, but if you want to make me happy you should."

For the Plaintiff, impeach the testimony of Post, utilizing the written or video transcript of her deposition, or both.